W9-BOO-234

Hand Analysis

The Diagnostic Method

Edo Sprong

Sterling Publishing Co., Inc.   New York

To Ghanshyam Singh Birla, Ph.D., who, with dedication and devotion, taught me this science and inspired me to develop it and disseminate it to others.

Illustrations: Flip Mulder

Layout: Hans Britsemmer

Translation and editing: Tony Burrett, TDS/Utrecht, The Netherlands

Translation edited by Laurel Ornitz

Library of Congress Cataloging-in-Publication Data

Sprong, Edo.
    [Handanalyse en zelfherkenning. English]
    Hand analysis : the diagnostic method / Edo Sprong.
       p.   cm.
    Translation of: Handanalyse en zelfherkenning.
    Includes index.
    ISBN 0-8069-8352-3
    1. Palmistry.   I. Title.
  BF928.D8S6713   1991
  133.5—dc20   91-3299
                                                 CIP

10 9 8 7 6 5 4 3 2

English translation © 1991 by Sterling Publishing Company
387 Park Avenue South, New York, N.Y. 10016
Original edition published under the title
Handanalyse en Zelfherkenning: Alles in de hand
© 1988 by Uitgeversmaatschappij, Tirion, Baarn
Distributed in Canada by Sterling Publishing
c/o Canadian Manda Group, P.O. Box 920, Station U
Toronto, Ontario, Canada M8Z 5P9
Distributed in Great Britain and Europe by Cassell PLC
Villiers House, 41/47 Strand, London WC2N 5JE
Distributed in Australia by Capricorn Ltd.
P.O. Box 665, Lane Cove, NSW 2066
Manufactured in the United States of America
All rights reserved

Sterling ISBN 0-8069-8352-3

CONTENTS

I wish to extend my heartfelt thanks to the Institut National de Recherche pour la Connaissance de Soi, Inc.—351 Victoria Avenue, Westmount, Quebec, Canada H23 2H1—for their kind permission to use material derived from the Institute.

INTRODUCTION

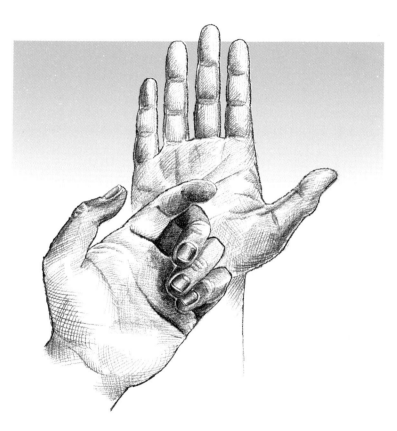

Diagnostic hand analysis is a fascinating science, and for this reason, I want to share my knowledge of it with others. This book is partly based on the ten-day basic course of the Academy of Anthropodynamics, an international school of diagnostic hand analysis, transpersonal therapy, and psychology, with headquarters in The Netherlands. I do not claim that this book is a complete survey of all aspects of hand analysis. That would be impossible, for diagnostic and evolutionary hand analysis is a complex subject that must be unravelled step by step. However, as the director of the Academy, the experience of many lectures and basic courses has shown me that people can both identify with and profit from the material presented here.

I ask you not to focus your attention too much on the negative qualities reflected in the hand, because compensations for these very qualities can often be "read" elsewhere in the hand. Perhaps you will feel offended, even annoyed, by the interpretation of a trait you are not yet ready to accept. If so, then it is important to think more deeply about it. The acceptance of our "dark side" is essential to our growth, because it is difficult to modify a negative quality if we ourselves do not first accept it. The concept of a dark side was introduced by the famous Swiss psychologist Dr. Carl Jung, who called the repressed negative traits the "shadow" or "dark side" of the ego personality.

The roots of freedom are encapsulated in the classic Delphic command "Man, know thyself." Self-knowledge is the first step towards overcoming our limitations and reaching maturity. Self-knowledge is also the basis of realizing our full potential.

THE CEREBRAL CORTEX MAN
Professor Penfield, a Canadian brain surgeon, localized the areas responsible for the transfer of information to various parts of the body by means of electrical stimulation of the motor section of the cerebral cortex.

It is striking that such a large area of this part of the brain is linked to the thumb, the fingers, and the hand.

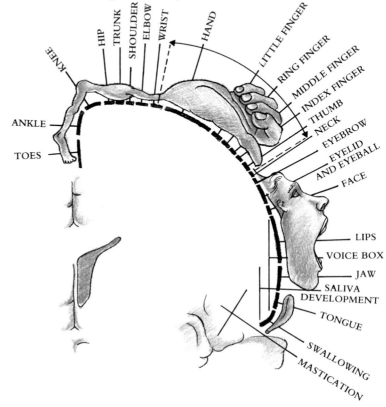

This hand analysis system is based on the Eastern doctrine of evolution, which encompasses the concept of reincarnation, a subject that appears from time to time in this book. In my practice, I see clients who have various religious views—views that I always respect and that I sometimes use to elucidate my advice. The application of this system, therefore, demands no belief in the concept of reincarnation. Such a belief merely provides another dimension in tracing underlying causes of blocks and may suggest a potential therapeutic approach. If a client rejects the concept of reincarnation, I speak about the essential character with which he or she was born.

On writing the chapter concerning mounts, I realized once again how complex this subject is and how difficult it can be to explain. However, by comparing hands, you will be able to recognize differences better and make more accurate assessments. The students at the Academy usually find this chapter the most difficult.

The philosopher Dr. Rudolph Steiner, the founder of anthroposophy, has written that in the future we will be able to detect whether others have the powers of, for example, Jupiter or Saturn, within them. Hand analysis provides an insight into such properties of character; in fact, many people believe its purpose is to become generally known in order to realize Steiner's prophccy.

I hope that this book contributes to that end. I also hope that this form of hand analysis gives you as much pleasure and benefit as it has given—and continues to give—my clients, my students, and myself.

EDO SPRONG

ACADEMY ANTHROPODYNAMICS

International school of diagnostic hand analysis, transpersonal therapy, and psychology.
Head Office:
Post box 1003
4801 BA Breda
The Netherlands

1·WHAT IS DIAGNOSTIC HAND ANALYSIS?

The knowledge inherent in diagnostic hand analysis on which this book is based stems from the science of *jyotish*, which in Sanskrit means "a system of knowledge that radiates light."

Jyotish is also the name of a Sanskrit text dating back to the Vedas of ancient India. Part of this text is the *Hasta Samudrika Shastra,* which can be translated as "a sea of knowledge concerning hand analysis." In both its teaching and application, diagnostic hand analysis encompasses this ancient science along with Western and Eastern philosophies and modern psychological, neurophysiological, cybernetic, and therapeutic concepts. This hand analysis method, which is systematically classified, can thus be seen as combining the spiritual psychology of the East with the psychological knowledge of the West.

Throughout the centuries, philosophers and psychologists have noted a relationship existing between physical characteristics and human character. For instance, Dr. Alexander Lowen, director of the Institute of Bioenergetic Analysis, has written that an individual is the totality of his or her life experiences and that these experiences are registered in the personality and in the structure of the body. Just as an expert can read the life history of a tree from its annual growth rings, so it is possible to detect personal information from the human body. Concerning hand analysis in particular, the famous Swiss psychologist Dr. Carl Jung wrote: "The hands, whose shape and functioning are so intimately connected with the psyche, might provide revealing and, therefore, interpretable expressions of psychical peculiarity, that is, of the human character."

Diagnostic hand analysis is based upon the person and is concerned with character analysis. The anticipation of future trends has a place in this science, but its signficance has more to do with providing an opportunity for learning and self-actualization than with deterministically predicting the future. Diagnostic hand analysis not only indicates which problems people have, but, even more importantly, indicates which facets of their character have caused these problems. This science demonstrates that all events fit into the total pattern of our lives. When we understand ourselves better, we become less likely to continuously repeat the same mistakes or to create negative situations. In this respect, this science is preventative rather than predictive. In no sense whatsoever, therefore, can diagnostic hand analysis be regarded simply as palmistry or fortune-telling.

Fatalism has no place in this method. The examination of the hand as a diagnostic method is set in the context of modern-day psychological knowledge. Based on this knowledge, we can modify future potential by changing our mental outlook. Moreover, if we are aware of the negative forces in our psyche and confront them, then they lose their power over us and we are thus in a position to make choices. If we are not aware of these forces, however, we give them the opportunity to dominate us.

Diagnostic hand analysis meets such definitions of science as "a well-founded certain knowledge" and "a systematic knowledge of reality." As with every scientific system, it is based on certain laws. The essence of diagnostic hand analysis is to interrelate all our functional activities with seven archetypes and seven hand types that represent specific spiritual, mental, emotional, and physical behavior patterns. Fingers, nails, skin patterns, mounts, lines, and other indications, together with the hand type, form a blueprint of our personality.

Applications

Diagnostic hand analysis has numerous applications. However, only a few will be briefly discussed here.

INSIGHT INTO THE PERSONALITY AND THE INNER PERSON

This involves evaluation of the character, with its behavioral and thought patterns, developed and latent qualities, harmonious and contending traits, strong and weak points, defense mechanisms, repressions, identifications, and underlying causes. Diagnostic hand analysis helps to explain how we can develop ourselves more fully, and how we can acquire self-confidence and remove blocks to our growth. Fundamental growth means broadening our boundaries outwardly (in perspective) and inwardly (in depth). The influence of the various stages in our life cycle is also illuminated.

DEVELOPMENT OF CHILDREN

Childhood is the best time to create a harmonious interaction between an individual and his or her environment because children are very receptive to influences of all kinds. Therapy can therefore be highly effective at this stage. The assessment of the physical, emotional, intellectual, and spiritual potential of children contributes to a deeper understanding of their talents, interests, disturbances, complexes, preferences, intelligence, and aptitudes.

By means of diagnostic hand analysis, the causes of learning difficulties can be diagnosed and possible remedies suggested. Counselling can also be given regarding the most suitable subjects to be studied and can provide the means by which a child can best be motivated.

FAMILY AND RELATIONSHIP COUNSELLING

Unnecessary tension can arise in families and relationships if unrecognized negative emotions control human behavior and consciousness.

The paradoxical adage "ill-matched is well-matched" is relevant here because it implies great opportunities for growth and in growth lies happiness. However, one source of difficulty is that partners often communicate from different unconscious perspectives, such as, for example, visual, emotional, or auditive perspectives. In these cases, a joint consultation or a mutual knowledge of hand analysis can be extremely fruitful.

It is important to have a mutual understanding of the conscious and unconscious motives that determine behavior, of the reactions they produce, and of how a relationship is influenced by them.

TRENDS AND FUTURE POTENTIAL

Indeed, the anticipation of future trends has a place in this science, but the accent lies more on how we ourselves can create our future in order to realize our potential than on our going through life with a fatalistic attitude.

SPIRITUAL DEVELOPMENT

In diagnostic hand analysis, attention is directed to the process of self-development. Based on pre- and postnatal tendencies, the science indicates how we can cultivate spiritual qualities, such as coordination of thought, harmonious activities, perseverance, tolerance, trust in our superconsciousness, inner balance, affectionate detachment, unselfish love, and creativity. An appropriate spiritual direction for the individual can be recommended.

VITAL EXISTENTIAL QUESTIONS

With the aid of this science, we can develop a better understanding of changing circumstances, inner impulses, and the meaning of present or past experiences. This enables us to better understand similar repetitive and painful experiences. Through this we in turn acquire insight into which misfortunes, adversities, oppositions, and conflicts we must overcome in order to grow spiritually, mentally, and emotionally. The purpose or the direction of life (the leitmotiv) can also be examined. Gaining an understanding of the meaning of life can have great powers of integration. Sometimes it is also possible with this method to eradicate neurotic patterns by means of reorientation.

HEALTH AND SEXUALITY

The main cause of poor health and sexual problems has to do with a disruption in the harmonious interrelation of spiritual, mental, emotional, and physical energies. This disruption can be seen in the hand long before it manifests itself physically. A symptom can even be a manifestation of certain emotions from the past, including previous incarnations, which have not been assimilated by the consciousness.

Every organ and part of the body is reflected in the hand. Through this science, therefore, it is possible to discover the sources of illnesses and sexual problems, and to either prevent them or promote the healing process.

CHOICE OF PROFESSION OR CAREER

In terms of choosing a career, diagnostic hand analysis can be used to offer advice, based on the skills, aptitudes, character, and experience of an individual.

SELECTION OF PERSONNEL

This science is a useful aid in the selection of personnel, as it can provide insight into the abilities, aptitudes, experience, potential, disposition, initiative, and temperament of the applicant. A character sketch can also be enriched by making use of a scientific interview technique or the model of physiognomy, based on the seven archetypes (see Chapter 6). In addition, business partners or future associates can profit from the insights offered by this system.

APPLICATIONS OF DIAGNOSTIC HAND ANALYSIS

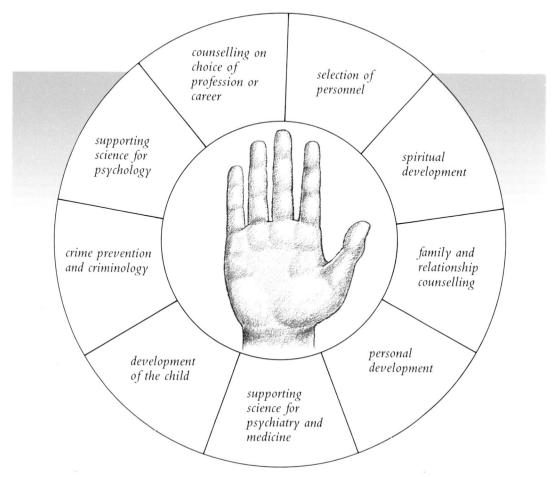

2·THE THUMB

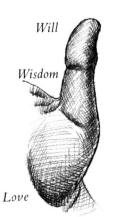

Will

Wisdom

Love

The thumb represents the human soul, whose three basic elements can be found in it. *Will* (willpower and determination) is established in the first phalanx of the thumb, *wisdom* (reason and logic) in the second, and *love* (feeling and sympathy) in the third, or the Mount of Venus (see the illustration). Since all emotions and human behavior are based on will, wisdom, and love, the thumb can furnish us with a great deal of information.

The thumb is also a symbol of the divine aspect of man. Isaac Newton, one of the founders of modern science, once said that if there were no other evidence, the thumb alone would convince him of the existence of God. The Trinity (Father, Son, and Holy Ghost) of Christianity and the three Gods (*Trimurti*) of Hinduism are symbolized by the thumb (see the illustration).

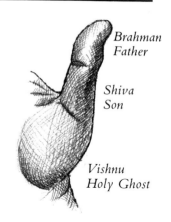

Brahman
Father

Shiva
Son

Vishnu
Holy Ghost

If we examine the thumb, we realize what a fascinating part of the hand it is. In fact, it can be said that the thumb is the most important part of the hand. Therefore, when we "read" someone's hand, we always look first at the thumb.

The thumb symbolizes our individuality and our capacity to speak, think, and feel, the abilities that distinguish us from animals. Apes, for example, have very short thumbs. They live according to their instincts and are not regarded as creatures with souls.

The thumb also shows how much a person is motivated to apply the three qualities of will, wisdom, and love in everyday life. The thumb can thus be seen as the base on which the whole hand rests. A "powerful" thumb indicates a basic ability to achieve something in life. This remains true even if other signs in the hand indicate the opposite.

The importance of the thumb can be illustrated with an example from my own practice.

I was once consulted by a woman whose whole hand expressed little motivation. However, she had an unusually long thumb. I put her under light hypnosis and called upon her thumb to exert control. From that moment on, her entire life changed.

We sometimes conceal our thumbs in our hands. This means that we are afraid to express our inner self. We will not stick our neck out and are somewhat afraid of the challenges of life. If we conceal our thumbs in our hands in cold weather, however, we are demonstrating a wish to retain our spirituality, or our "inner warmth."

Through its symbolism, the folktale about Tom Thumb sheds light on the importance of the thumb. Most of us remember the story of the little fellow who, together with his six brothers, was abandoned in the forest because his father could no longer support his family.

The first time they were left in the forest, Tom was able to lead his brothers home by leaving a trail of pebbles. The second time, he left a trail of breadcrumbs, but they were eaten by hungry birds, and the brothers lost their way in the dark forest. But, still, Tom Thumb did not lose heart. Cleverly, he stole the giant's seven-league boots and, with them, brought his brothers safely home.

The three basic elements of the thumb are convincingly demonstrated by Tom Thumb's behavior. The little fellow had the desire (will) to bring his brothers home. Moreover, he had the determination to march in the giant's seven-league boots. He thought (wisdom) of various ways of finding his way home, such as leaving pebbles and breadcrumbs, and he was so fond of his brothers (love) that he refused to abandon them. We can also compare the six brothers with the six hand shapes (see Chapter 5). The thumb leads, as it were, these six hand shapes through the evolutionary process, as Tom Thumb led his brothers through the uncertainties of life and brought them safely back home.

Sucking our thumb also has a particular meaning, namely, that we are attempting to stimulate our will (the first phalanx). We should not disturb a baby sucking his thumb, because by so doing, he is trying to summon his willpower.

The Length of the Thumb

The length of the thumb is of the greatest importance because from this we can determine various qualities. To measure the thumb, we lay the hand flat, palm upwards. The thumb should be relaxed and pushed in towards the index (Jupiter) finger. We then draw a line across the midpoint of the third phalanx of this finger and note where the top of the thumb lies in relation to it (see the illustration).

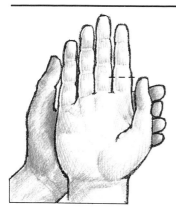
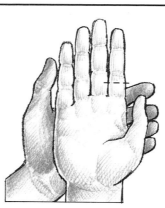

Normal length   *Short thumb*   *Long thumb*

NORMAL LENGTH

If the top of the thumb reaches the line exactly, then the thumb is of normal length. There is a certain balance between being under- and overmotivated, and people with this type of thumb thus possess average motivation.

SHORT THUMB

If the top of the thumb does not reach the line, then we speak of a "short thumb." People with such thumbs need a kick in the pants! They should show more motivation and get on with their life. Such people are often fatalistic and sit around waiting to see what comes along. But sitting still in effect means going backwards, which is not the intention in life. People with short thumbs must stimulate themselves or be stimulated by others more.

LONG THUMB

When the top of the thumb lies above the line, then we speak of a "long thumb." People with long thumbs are very motivated to lead a productive life. They have the innate ability to achieve something. If the top of the thumb lies too far above the line, however, then there is a danger of an excess of motivation. Often these people are so determined to manifest themselves that they impose their will on others. "Keeping someone under the thumb" is then an appropriate saying.

It sometimes occurs that the thumb of the right hand is shorter than that of the left. This can indicate that in the past (meaning, in a previous life), that person had a very unpleasant experience. Their reincarnated soul now desires to "take it easy." The problem, however, is that life does not allow us simply to lay down our burden and take it easy. It forces us to take action and to learn lessons from the unpleasant things that happen to us.

There are indications of improvement when the right thumb is longer than the left. Rather than taking it easy, we have decided to exercise more willpower and focus our exertions on developing our abilities and fulfilling our potential.

The Position of the Thumb

Not only the length, but also the position (or setting) of the thumb is of importance.

As mentioned earlier, the thumb represents man's soul. This means that the thumb reflects the higher realms in man, in contrast to the palm, which shows how we handle events in everyday life.

If the hand is relaxed, we can see that the thumb rests naturally at a particular angle to the rest of the hand.

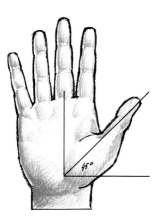

NORMAL POSITION

If the thumb forms an angle of approximately 45° with the hand (see the illustration), then we use our inner power in a balanced manner. It could be said that we are in equilibrium between introversion and extroversion.

CLOSE TO THE HAND

It can also occur, of course, that the thumb is carried close to the hand (see the illustration). This indicates caution. These people are afraid to be open. They distance themselves from the challenges and opportunities of life. They dare not face the world head-on and tend to remain in their shells.

People who carry the thumb very close to the hand have never developed a real personality of their own. These people tend to do what others think they should do or want them to do. They tend to be henpecked and should try to change this situation.

They must cut the umbilical cord. It can be stated categorically that such people have never grown up. If this sounds too harsh, these people can nevertheless be comforted with the thought that they still have many good qualities and there is no reason why they shouldn't make the most of them. These people must be encouraged and convinced of their own capabilities.

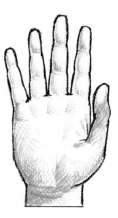

FAR FROM THE HAND

Another possibility is that the thumb is set well away from the hand. This indicates an unconscious longing for the spaciousness of the cosmos.

This is a commendable aspiration, but one that nonetheless conceals a danger. In terms of human behavior, people with such thumbs tend to overestimate their own abilities. They try to achieve too much and run the risk of taking on too much. They cherish a desire to do "great things." This is fine as long as everything is going well, but when they are faced with setbacks they become frustrated. People with thumbs like this, therefore, must hold back to some extent, and are advised to reflect on their human limitations before they plunge into "life's sea of troubles."

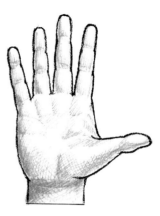

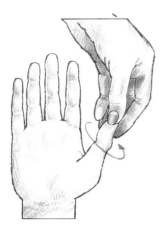

The Mobility of the Thumb

How can we discover if the thumb is mobile? The right hand is relaxed and the thumb is taken in the fingers of the left hand. It is now rotated slowly and we observe whether it resists or moves freely (see the illustration).

SUPPLE THUMB

People whose thumb rotates in a supple, or flexible, way are also flexible in their behavior. Their outlook on life is elastic, and they can take its blows without flinching. In short, they have a balanced nature and tend to strike the happy medium.

LOOSE THUMB

If the thumb appears to be almost loose in its socket and can be rotated in all directions, then we speak of a "loose-jointed thumb" (see the illustration).

People with such thumbs are not usually single-minded or persevering. They do not know what they want, because they are not well-grounded and have no deep roots. Because of this, they find it difficult to form their own opinions. They tend to go where the wind blows and are easy to influence. If an actor has a loose-jointed thumb, for example, it indicates his gift for taking on the character of another, because he is not deeply rooted in his own character. However, if such people do form an opinion, they tend to cling to it desperately. Sometimes they also become somewhat arrogant or cocky, from a fear of having to begin the process of forming an opinion again.

People with a loose-jointed thumb must learn to listen to themselves more often and to believe that their opinion has just as much worth as that of another.

STIFF THUMB

People with a stiff thumb are usually dependable and have an objective view of life. But they can also be obstinate. It is fine to have your own opinion, but sticking to it inflexibly is not always a good thing. Think of a deeply rooted, unbending tree. It cannot sway in the wind and if the wind reaches storm force, the tree snaps like a twig. For this reason, in Taoism the bamboo is regarded as the ideal tree, because not only can it stand upright, but it is also extremely flexible and bends easily.

The thumb can be given a certain mobility by exercise and this favorably influences the flexibility of the character. The more supple the thumb, the less obstinately we behave. This applies to the whole hand. When the hand or part of the hand becomes stiff after an accident, for example, it is nature's message telling us to behave in a more flexible manner.

The French sculptor César also sees the thumb as a tree rooted in the earth. (Photo courtesy of Beeldrecht, Amsterdam.)

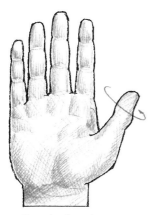

Supple thumb

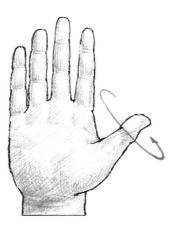

Loose thumb

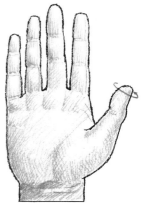

Stiff thumb

The Phalanges of the Thumb

If the three basic elements of the thumb—will, wisdom, and love—are not in balance, the innate harmony between these faculties is disturbed. We are at our happiest in life when these three elements are in balance.

Indications concerning potential disharmony can be found in the phalanges of the thumb. A phalanx is part of a finger (or toe) and is demarcated by a fold or crease in the skin. A thumb that is out of balance does not necessarily indicate disaster—at least not if we are prepared to work on our further development.

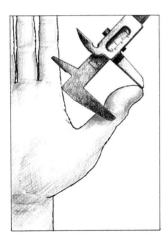

Measuring the Phalanges

The phalanges of the thumb can be measured with a graduated rule or vernier calipers. When counting phalanges, we always begin from the end of the digit. The first phalanx runs from the tip of the thumb to the crease. The second phalanx runs from the crease to the place where the thumb meets the hand, which is also marked by a crease.

EQUAL LENGTH

If the phalanges are of equal length, then we have achieved a balance between the three elements (see the illustration).

FIRST PHALANX (WILL) LONGER

If we observe that the first phalanx (will) is longer than the second (wisdom) (see the illustration), then we probably desire a great deal but do not always think carefully about our desires. We tend to behave impulsively (which is not the same thing as behaving spontaneously). The saying "Look before you leap" is applicable here.

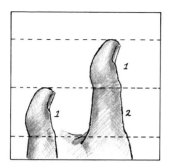

Equal length

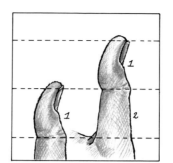

*First phalanx longer,
second phalanx shorter*

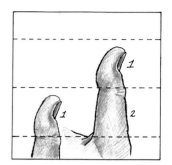

*Second phalanx longer,
first phalanx shorter*

People whose first phalanx is extra long are fairly ego-centric and they continually attempt to impose their point of view on others. The obverse of this is that they can also be very susceptible to flattery. Others stroke their ego and in so doing impose their point of view on them.

Such a person could, for example, have been the owner of a large plantation in a previous life. Without any exertion on his part, he led a life of ease and luxury. His extra long phalanx means that by making demands in this life, he thinks he will again get everything his heart desires.

Because of his demanding nature, he encounters opposition in his everyday life. Therefore, he must learn to exert himself more on his own behalf. Life does not owe him a living.

SECOND PHALANX (WISDOM) LONGER

People with a long second phalanx (wisdom) (see the illustration) are generally good at making plans but not so good at putting them into effect. These people do a great deal of reasoning but then do nothing, because their will is not sufficiently developed.

"Armchair philosophers," for example, may have a long second phalanx. People with a long second phalanx are advised to develop more perseverance. Making plans is all very well, but putting those plans into action is what counts.

THIRD PHALANX

The third phalanx (love) of the thumb is the Mount of Venus. This will be discussed in Chapter 6.

The Thumb Shapes

As mentioned earlier, the thumb is the most fascinating part of the hand. Not only can we derive information from its length, but we can also derive information from its shape.

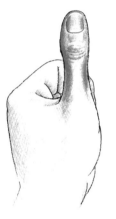

THE WAISTED THUMB

If the second phalanx (wisdom) of the thumb is waistlike (see the illustration), then this can indicate particularly diplomatic behavior. The qualities of reason and logic are refined by the constriction and we achieve our goals by saying the right things in the right way. Although this can be a positive gift, it, too, has a flip side. Diplomacy can become manipulation. But since all manifestations of life contain virtue as well as vice, manipulation with good motives can be viewed as positive. Manipulation with devious motives (to the exclusive benefit of ourselves), however, is negative, and perhaps in these cases we should modify our behavior.

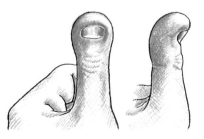

THE CLUBBED THUMB

In a clubbed thumb (see the illustration) the top of the first phalanx (will) is unusually broad. The quality of the will is corrupted, as it were, and can degenerate into malice. People with a clubbed thumb may have suppressed rage in their subconscious mind that manifests itself in their contact with other people. They may, for example, project their own suppressed anger onto others and attribute their own vices (of which they may not be aware) to them. This accusatory attitude can be so powerful that it is reflected back. People with clubbed thumbs, therefore, are often confronted with the anger of others and have absolutely no idea why. But, in fact, it is the reflection of their own suppressed anger. Such people are not "bad"; rather, they have a deeply hidden block that could probably be relieved by a qualified therapist.

I know a man who has a clubbed thumb on only his left hand. This indicates that in a previous life, he was able to overcome cruelty and coarseness, since the clubbed thumb on his right hand is no longer present.

In my practice I met a woman with a hand like a Madonna, except for a huge club thumb. Using regression therapy (that is, returning to the past), I was able to discover that she had suffered terribly in a previous life. This was the reason for her great suppressed anger. I applied a particular therapy and after a time her club thumb dwindled. And from then on, her life was also much more peaceful.

THE NOBLE THUMB

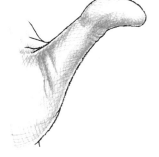

Now look once again closely at the first phalanx of your thumb. If this phalanx bends back (see the illustration), then you have what we call a "noble thumb."

As mentioned earlier, the hand itself can be compared with the material world, with everyday life. However, the first phalanx of this thumb is clearly not interested and turns away from the world of matter.

People with such a thumb are often generous and have a tendency to give their possessions away. However, when this positive quality is taken to the extreme and becomes self-sacrifice, we are in effect denying ourselves, and that can be very foolish. Indeed, it can be most unpleasant if a storm breaks and we have no roof over our head. In terms of noble behavior, it is probably best to develop a sense of reality, to tread the middle path.

During one of my lectures, a woman with such a thumb was in the audience. She could not recognize the behavioral pattern because for her it was perfectly normal. But as I was talking, her husband sat nodding vigorously in agreement.

THE OBLATE THUMB

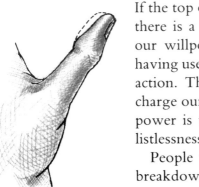

If the top of our thumb is not rounded but feels flat, then there is a void (see the illustration). This indicates that our willpower is exhausted. This can be the result of having used up "nervous" energy or lacking concentrated action. The available power is fragmented and we discharge our energies with no clear aim in view. Our willpower is undermined by the wasted use of energy and listlessness results.

People with this type of thumb often suffer nervous breakdowns. As a prevention, they must try to be calmer and to use their energy in a more balanced way. Naturally, an oblate thumb can also be the consequence of diminishing energy in advanced age.

The Shape of the Thumb Tips

Just as the shape of the top part of the thumb gives us clues about our personality, the shape of the thumb tip can also supply important information.

CONIC TIP

A conic (cone-shaped) thumb tip (see the illustration) means that we behave spontaneously. Often influences are taken to heart and we express ourselves without sufficient thought beforehand. Many artists and writers probably have such thumb tips.

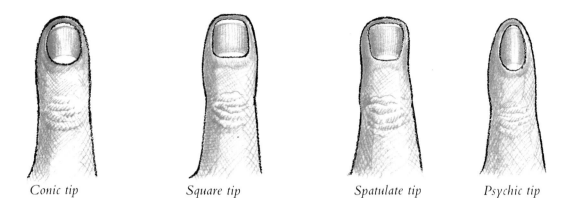

Conic tip *Square tip* *Spatulate tip* *Psychic tip*

SQUARE TIP

A square thumb tip (see the illustration) is an indication of a more efficient use of energy. Therefore, people with square thumb tips usually are practical by nature and think carefully before they act. Sometimes they are also rather skeptical.

SPATULATE TIP

A thumb tip is spatulate if the first phalanx is slightly waisted (see the illustration). People with this tip are un-usually dynamic. They have an enterprising nature and an adventurous pioneering spirit. They use their energy in a dynamic way.

PSYCHIC TIP

People with such a pointed tip (see the illustration) act intuitively, rarely pausing for thought. If they really want to succeed, however, then they must learn to use their reasoning abilities. They must also learn to keep at least one foot on the ground.

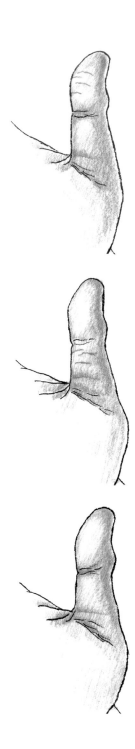

Transverse Lines on the Thumb

All the lines that run transversely across the hand indicate frustrations. The thinner and shorter these lines are, the smaller the frustrations. Thick, long lines, on the other hand, indicate deep frustrations. This also applies to transverse lines on the thumb.

TRANSVERSE LINES ON THE FIRST PHALANX

If there are transverse lines on the first phalanx on the inside of the thumb turning towards the index finger (see the illustration), then we are experiencing frustrations in the expression of our *will*. We want to do something, but we are hindered from doing it. The transverse lines indicate that the energy is blocked.

TRANSVERSE LINES ON THE SECOND PHALANX

As was explained earlier, the second phalanx of the thumb has to do with *wisdom* and represents our powers of reasoning. Transverse lines on this phalanx thus signify frustrations in regard to our logical thinking.

When something happens in our life, we attempt to figure out why it has happened. We think and think but cannot come up with the answer. This can create a particular type of frustration that is visible in the wisdom phalanx of our thumb. If the lines on the phalanges are thin, they may disappear as soon as our current frustrations are over. Thick, deeply etched lines, however, indicate a permanent feeling of frustration. I invite you to consider the hypothesis that if we create our own impediments ourselves, we can also remove them ourselves.

NOTE

We must not confuse the lines of frustration on the wisdom phalanx with the catenary curve (see the illustration) by the root of the thumb and the lines that lie close to it. These have a different meaning.

3·FINGERS AND NAILS

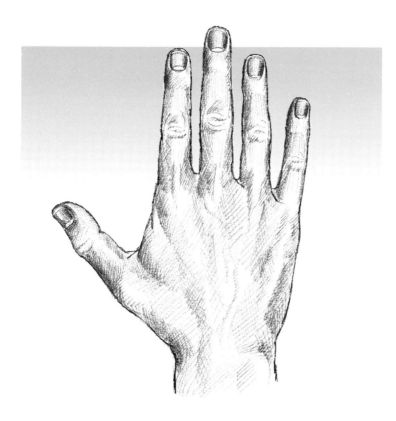

Our fingers are naturally used for gripping things, but, in addition, they reveal a great deal about the personality structure of an individual. In the hand as a whole, the fingers represent the expression of conscious energy. This is the energy we need in order to cope with everyday life and to be able to function in a "normal" way.

Conversely, the palm of the hand represents unconscious energy. Many great philosophers and psychologists, such as Spinoza, Freud, and Jung, have expressed the belief that it is our unconscious energy that actually motivates us and determines our behavior.

To put it simply, we could regard the palm of the hand as a storehouse of energy with the fingers taking what

Smooth   *Knotty*

they need from it. In other words, the fingers tell us how in life we use the qualities stored within our being.

Smooth or Knotty Fingers

If we observe our fingers (or those of someone else), we can see that each finger has two knuckles. One of them is at the end of the first phalanx just below the nail and the other is at the end of the second phalanx.

Now we take the fingers of one hand in the fingers of the other and feel the sides and the top of the knuckles (see the illustration), noticing whether they are thick or thin. If the knuckles are thick, we speak of "knotty" fingers; if they are thin, we speak of "smooth" fingers.

If we have fairly smooth fingers, we have a tendency to act spontaneously. The fingers represent the emanation of our conscious energy, and if this energy is not impeded, as it were, by the knuckles, it is able to flow out freely.

Conversely, people with knotty fingers tend to be cautious. Their energy flows out less easily and they think and act in an analytical manner.

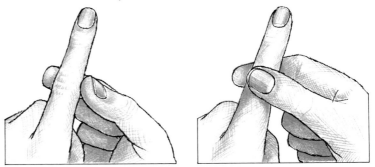

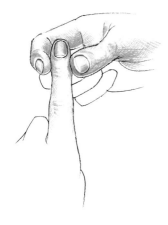

THICK UPPER KNUCKLE

The first finger joint (the upper knuckle) represents the mental, or intellectual, approach to life. A thick upper knuckle thus indicates a positive intellectual approach to life.

A married woman who has such a knuckle would

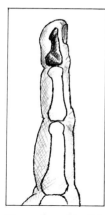 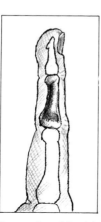 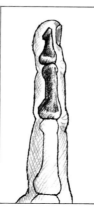

Upper knuckle thick   Lower knuckle thick   Both upper and lower
                                              knuckles thick

probably prefer to have a mentally stimulating job rather than spending her time doing housework. On the other hand, she can organize her housework so that everything runs like clockwork.

THICK LOWER KNUCKLE

The second finger joint (the lower knuckle) represents the practical approach to life. People who have thick lower knuckles, for example, would probably prefer to spend their time gardening or decorating the house rather than reading a dissertation on the origins of the universe.

BOTH UPPER AND LOWER KNUCKLES THICK

The upper and lower knuckles can both be thick, and if so, this indicates a balance between the intellectual and practical approaches.

Of course, society needs both "theoretical" and "practical" people. But it is still better if both manifestations are somewhat in balance in each individual.

It should be noted, however, that in all people the upper knuckle is always thinner than the lower knuckle (see the illustration, top right).

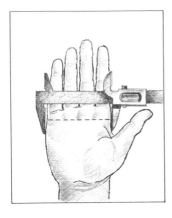

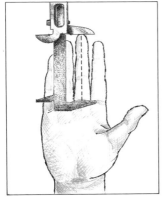

The Length of the Fingers

The length of the fingers is measured as follows. The hand is held flat with the fingers together. A graduated rule or vernier calipers is laid across the hand, just below the fingers, and the distance is measured (see the illustration).

The length of the middle finger (the finger of Saturn) is then measured. If the length of this finger is exactly the same as the width of the hand, the length of the fingers is normal and there is a balance between caution and rashness.

We speak of "short" fingers or "long" fingers if there is a difference between the length of the middle finger and the width of the hand. Long fingers indicate an analytical, intellectual capacity; short fingers indicate impetuosity.

SHORT SMOOTH FINGERS

In general, people with this type of finger cannot keep their mind on one thing for long. They do not allow themselves time to think things through and tend to say the first thing that comes to mind. They are very impulsive and should take care not to act too thoughtlessly.

They jump from one subject to another and can see no fixed direction in their future. They often feel unhappy because they have no firm base in life. "Look before you leap" is good advice for these people.

SHORT KNOTTY FINGERS

In general, people with this type of finger are quick thinkers, but the knuckles hold back the energy long enough for them to reach the right decisions.

Of course, this is an excellent quality for people in professions that require fast, accurate reactions to particular situations. Such people, for example, make excellent military officers, negotiators, or managers of production departments.

LONG SMOOTH FINGERS

People with this type of finger are contemplative, though not excessively so.

LONG KNOTTY FINGERS

People with long knotty fingers usually have a philosophical streak. In addition, they can be very good at making plans and solving problems. Solving crossword puzzles or playing chess are very likely among their greatest pleasures.

On a recent train journey, the conductor who checked my ticket had such fingers. The other passengers might just as well not have been there because for most of the journey we were deeply engaged in profound conversation.

The Nails

Nerves can be regarded as "thought carriers" and many of them end in the tips of our fingers. Our nails protect these nerve ends and therefore, in fact, our brain. (As we all know, the flesh under the fingernails is very sensitive.) Nails can give an indication of our physical, mental, and emotional health.

BROAD NAILS

Broad nails (see the illustration) indicate good physical health. People with broad nails often have a broad outlook on life as well. They are receptive to new points of view. They are also usually extroverted, cheerful, spontaneous, and persevering.

However, those whose nails are very broad and also flat (see the illustration) generally stick to their own point of view. They have fixed opinions and are self-willed and obstinate. Such people are seldom welcome participants in discussion groups!

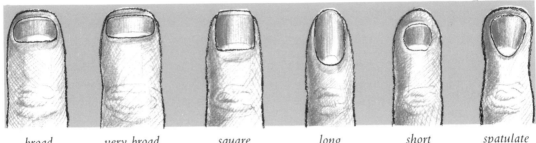

broad   very broad   square   long   short   spatulate

SQUARE NAILS

People with square nails (see the illustration) are practical and have a healthy interest in life and a healthy curiosity about the things that surround them.

This shape is a "diamond" among nail shapes because the three qualities of *will, wisdom,* and *love* are in a harmonious balance. In addition, people with square nails usually enjoy good health.

LONG NAILS

People with long nails (see the illustration) are usually delicately built. In general, their physical condition is not particularly strong.

These people tend to like an inner and outer harmony and beauty. They are fond of art, music, painting, and everything to do with design and decoration. Women with such nails, for example, can often be found working in beauty salons. They not only wish to appear well-groomed themselves but also take great delight in making others "beautiful." People with long nails are also often attracted to meditation groups.

SHORT NAILS

Short nails (see the illustration) connote less strong and robust health and a very critical mind. These people are analytical in thought and interested in the details of life.

There are disadvantages to being critical and meticulous, however. People who regard themselves critically have a tendency to criticize others as well. Being over-critical is not healthy. If we are too critical of ourselves, we also run the risk of continually condemning ourselves. The art lies in forgiving oneself, and in so doing, becoming less judgmental of others.

Such critical attitudes serve accountants and tax officials, among others. But such people should attempt to leave these attitudes behind in the office and not take them home with them—at least that would be more pleasant for their families.

SPATULATE NAILS

People with these nails (see the illustration) have a tendency to be nervous and to act nervously. They strive for perfection but almost never achieve it, which is why they are so nervous!

People with spatulate nails can do themselves a service by observing well-balanced and tranquil people and taking them as role models. A positive environment is also important, because in it they can more readily use their energy to fulfil their aspirations and desires without being impatient and nervous.

Equanimity of spirit is easier to maintain if we realize that tomorrow the sun will rise again, even if everything has gone completely wrong for us today!

4·THE HAND

Left- and Right-Handedness and Other Properties of the Hand

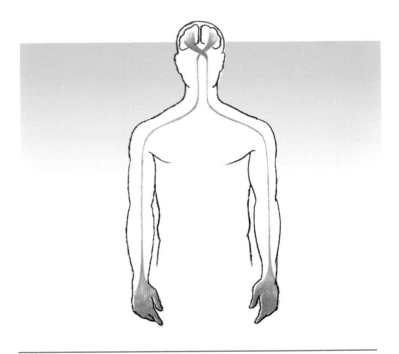

The left hand is controlled by the right half of the brain, which is associated with intuition, creativity, and timelessness. The right hand is controlled by the left half of the brain, associated with intellect, practicality, and time orientation.

The question I am most often asked is, which hand do I read: the left hand or the right? I will try to explain.

The upper main part of the brain (the cerebrum) is divided into left-hand and right-hand hemispheres, resembling two half-balls, with each representing a different pole of thought. The left cerebral hemisphere controls the right hand and the right cerebral hemisphere controls the left hand (see the illustration).

In left-handed people, the right hemisphere—the yin pole, according to Taoism—is dominant. This half of the brain is associated with intuition, creativity, receptivity, and introversion, and it is mostly related to the quality of *love*. The mode of thinking is timeless and holistic.

In right-handed people, the left hemisphere—the yang

pole in Taoism—is dominant. This half is associated with practical awareness and extroversion, and the mode of thinking is time-oriented. The left hemisphere controls our everyday life and the qualities of *will* and *wisdom* are most closely related to it.

The left hand shows hereditary factors, emotional experiences from childhood, and the sum of all experiences undergone in previous lives. The right hand shows our potential for this life. We can also say that the left hand shows what we are, and the right hand shows what we could be.

I always read both hands, but in left-handed people I pay more attention to the left hand and in right-handed people I pay more attention to the right.

Neither of the cerebral hemispheres is completely dominant in any individual: Everybody uses both. As far as hand analysis is concerned, it is important to decide to what extent the client uses his or her left hand. One way to discover this is to inquire! If a person was forced to write with the right hand in childhood, that does not necessarily make that person right-handed. There is a good deal more to say about this subject, but in such a basic book as this these are the clearest indications I can give.

I will add, however, that from my own experience, I know that in general left-handed people are more emotional than right-handed people. Left-handed people use the right hemisphere to control their everyday life and this side of the brain is not actually intended for that purpose. My conclusions were further validated by research conducted by the University of Michigan. Of the one thousand people who were questioned, the left-handers of both sexes judged themselves to be more emotional than the right-handers.

The Flexibility of the Hand

In a sense the flexibility of the hand is connected with the mobility of the thumb. Just as the mobility of the thumb tells us something about the flexibility of the will, so the flexibility of the fingers tells us something about the flexibility of our whole being—and therefore something about the flexibility of our actions.

The flexibility of the hand indicates to what extent we are open to outside influences, other ideas, and new impulses.

Whether a hand is flexible or not can be determined by bending back the fingers (see the illustration).

VERY FLEXIBLE HAND

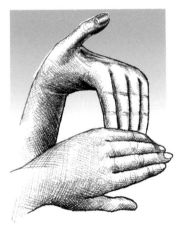

If we can push the fingers far back, then we probably have an elastic mind. We are open to other opinions and act upon them. If we can push the fingers very far back, however, we are probably too open to outside influences. We are quickly swayed and perhaps too compliant. If we always go along with the views of others, we may well lose sight of our own views. That can create confusion within ourselves, and also within others. We go where the wind blows us, we are fickle, and this creates an untrustworthy image.

INFLEXIBLE HAND

People with such a hand are not very open to the views of others. They often have rather inflexible minds and stick rigidly to their own ideas and opinions. They must take care that they do not adopt an attitude that is too stiff and uncompromising. What is required here is more responsiveness to the opinions of others and a greater flexibility of mind.

THE CRAMPED HAND

We sometimes see a hand in which the fingers are bent inward in an almost clawlike manner (see the illustration). This indicates great reserve and reticence. People with such hands are afraid of the challenges of life. They dare not adopt new ideas but adhere exclusively to old ones. Old sores and frustrations are fostered, often resulting in an extremely cramped way of life.

These people can try to make their minds more flexible by exercising the hands and bending the fingers back. It is well known that the brain directs the fingers (and much more), but many people still have to come to the realization that flexible fingers lead to a flexible mind.

Children's hands are unusually flexible, because children are completely open to all their impulses and to all the influences of life. If we look at the hand of an older person, however, then we often notice that it is beginning to stiffen. But this can easily be prevented by remaining mentally active and maintaining an interest in the changing world.

The Temperature of the Hands

The temperature of the hands can also yield information about ourselves or others. In general, we can say that warm hands indicate extroverted behavior and intensity. Conversely, cold hands indicate introverted behavior and subdued energy. The temperature of the hands is not necessarily constant and it can quickly change.

WARM HANDS

People with warm hands should consider themselves fortunate. They generally have good physical health and a healthy outlook on life. They coordinate their energy and actions very well and live in a harmonious manner.

HOT HANDS

People with hot hands possess an unusually large amount of bodily energy. This can be termed "get-up-and-go energy" and is by and large physically directed and not spiritual in nature. These people usually live intensely and involve themselves in activities with great passion and commitment. However, other people sometimes feel stifled by such intensity and become irritated with them.

COLD HANDS

People with cold hands often have a tendency to withdraw into themselves. Frequently there is an element of anxiety behind this withdrawal; they are afraid to "throw" themselves into life. Their get-up-and-go energy is largely extinguished. They feel a great deal of love, but in a gentle manner. They are often sensitive and recognize sincere emotions. The adage "Cold hands, warm heart" is an appropriate expression for them. With much tact and patience, one can bring these sensitive people back into the mainstream of life. This must not be done harshly, otherwise they will crawl back into their shells.

These people must learn to communicate better, both physically and emotionally.

PERSPIRING HANDS

As we all probably know, perspiring hands are usually a sign of nervousness and tension. We find ourselves in a particular situation, or must perform a certain act, that causes us anxiety, and our hands perspire. For example, at a job interview we want to present ourselves in the best way possible. We attempt to remain "cool," but we are far from it and therefore our hands sweat! In these situations it is best to keep in mind the words of Jesus: "Do not worry about tomorrow, sufficient are the problems of today."

The Skin Textures of the Hands

The skin of our hands also provides an indication of the manner in which we approach life. Our skin, indeed, is our first contact with the world. The skin of our hands serves to give us a grip on all the various tools and implements so that they do not slip through our fingers. In a metaphorical sense, the skin reveals the grip we have on the surrounding world. In short, it reveals how we deal with life. Skin patterns can be felt with the fingers or studied under a magnifying glass.

FINE SKIN TEXTURE

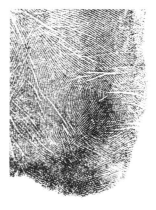

People with a fine skin texture usually have refined taste and therefore often have an interest in things like melodious music and paintings in pastel colors. This penchant for refinement, however, must not degenerate into a longing for an aimless life of luxury. The decadent life-style of the court of King Louis XIV of France is a striking example of such degeneration.

Most of us are not in a position to permit ourselves such a life-style, however; fortunately, the realities of life force us to exert effort and self-discipline.

COARSE SKIN TEXTURE

People with such a skin texture probably have a firm grip on the material side of life. But, conversely, they may have great difficulty in expressing their deeper feelings or dealing with other people in a kind and gentle manner. The expression "a rough diamond" can be applied to these people.

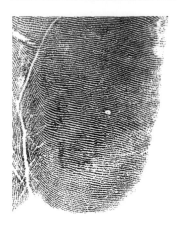

AVERAGE SKIN TEXTURE

People with this skin texture have the best of both worlds. They can be both efficient and practical as well as sensitive to their surroundings.

The Elasticity of the Palm

This concerns the resilience or springiness of the palm. To "measure" its elasticity, we press the fingers quite firmly into the palm and feel whether the flesh is elastic, hard, or soft. We also observe whether the flesh springs back as soon as the pressure is released.

The palm of the hand can be compared to a ball. If we press a football, we can feel that it is very hard with barely any "give." Conversely, if we press a beach ball, we feel that it is softer and offers much less resistance. In general, it can be said that the elasticity of the palm reflects our attitude towards life.

HARD PALM

Let us consider again the example of a ball. Everything bounces off a hard football and, in the same way, everything "bounces off" people with hard palms. They reject everything outside themselves. They resist responding to life, which can be the result of deep-rooted fear.

They are often insensitive to outside influences. They barely admit their existence, let alone react to it. All in all, they are not very interested in the emotions of others and tend to be uncaring, obstinate, and stubborn.

Usually these people have no interest in physical comfort.

In my practice I have often come across the situation in which one partner in a marriage complains that the other partner does not respond to his or her romantic overtures. If I press the palms of both partners, I frequently find that the unresponsive partner has a hard palm.

SOFT PALM

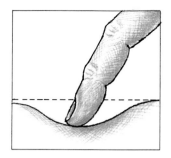

People with soft palms do not reject others, but they have no "springiness" to their nature. We can compare their behavior with that of a soft ball, which hardly bounces back at all. These people react in much the same way. They are friendly and pleasant, but they have no resilience. They do react to emotions, but then do not do very much more about them. They tend to bottle things up—so much so that sometimes it leads to illness.

In addition, these people tend to enjoy physical comfort and seek out a peaceful existence. But if this peacefulness is founded in softness, it is not a real inner peace. We only attain this when we have taken the lessons of life to heart. The meaning of life is to develop ourselves, which can only be done if we accept life's challenges.

ELASTIC PALM: NORMAL PALM

People with such palms face life with resilience and tolerance. They have a positive attitude towards life. The adage "give and take" is highly appropriate here.

The Color of the Hand

You have probably never looked so much at your hands or those of others as you have while reading these chapters. But there is still more to come, because the color of the skin also yields important information.

To determine the color of the hands, we examine the palms.

PINK

A pink palm indicates a jolly, cheerful attitude towards life. One's blood circulation is healthy and one's state of mind is generally harmonious.

RED

People with red palms have a great deal of energy. They are very pushy and do not often let themselves be thwarted. They are "doers" and can boast of an iron constitution.

It often occurs, however, that this energy is transposed into sensuality and uncontrolled emotional outbursts. This happens, for example, when circumstances interfere with the realization of their wishes.

YELLOW

A yellow coloration can indicate that the blood lacks vitality. It can also mean that the liver is not functioning as it should.

Because people with yellowish palms have little energy and are therefore often tired, they cannot do everything they might wish to do. This causes them to become first irritated and then disappointed, which can lead to feelings of depression.

WHITE

White hands connote an extreme exhaustion of energy. If the hands are both white and cold, this can indicate that the adrenal glands are exhausted. The causes are probably wrong diet, stress, or overwork. Sometimes the white coloration is the result of a temporary fright or shock. In this case, the blood drains away from the face and hands in order to defend the system elsewhere. Someone might remark, "You look like you've seen a ghost!" People with white hands often have difficulty imagining a hopeful future.

If we want to help these people, we must give them hope and encourage them to adopt an optimistic attitude. We must be very careful not to push them even further down by criticizing them.

5·HAND SHAPES

The different hand shapes reflect the evolutionary process of man. As many of you probably know, we can only develop by undergoing a process of growth. This growth process can be recognized in the hand shapes—from the elementary hand to the psychic hand.

In the chapter concerning the thumb, I described how the thumb represents the basic motivation of an individual to apply the three qualities of *will, wisdom,* and *love* in this life. These qualities can also be recognized in the hand shapes. The shape of the hand—the palm and the fingers—denotes the basic structure of our character, the basic qualities we have within us. The mounts (which will be discussed in the following chapter) show how we handle these qualities and how we apply them in our daily life. We could say, therefore, that the qualities indicated by the shape of the hand and by the mounts, together with the lines that connect the mounts, determine our behavior. In addition to the six different basic hand shapes, there is a seventh, which we call the "mixed" shape. The six hand shapes were mentioned in the tale of Tom Thumb, in which they were represented by his six brothers.

It is essential to understand that it is a rare occurrence to find a "pure" hand shape. Almost everyone has a "mixed" hand shape, and so we look for the shape that dominates the others. For example, if an individual has a hand that is 60 percent square and 40 percent conic, then the square hand shape is regarded as the main type.

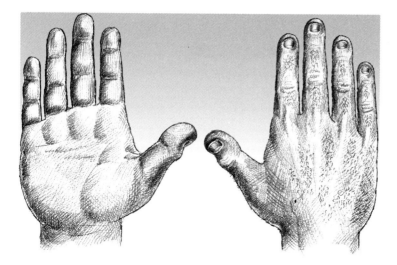

The Elementary Hand

PHYSICAL CHARACTERISTICS OF THE ELEMENTARY HAND

When we look closely at the elementary hand (see the illustration), we see that the skin texture is rather rough. Usually the back of the hand is hairy and these hairs are generally coarse and curly.

The palm often feels hard. The color is often on the red side, which indicates a great deal of energy. Elementary hands almost always feel warm, which also points to a great deal of physical energy.

The thumb is short: The motivation to achieve something in life is usually lacking. The lower phalanges of the fingers, which relate to the bodily aspect, are thick, so people with these hands tend to be physically oriented. They are usually well-muscled and can summon great physical power. The finger phalanges of the elementary hand are irregular and are not in harmony with each other.

The lines in the hand are broad and shallow.

The elementary hand is strongly associated with the basic quality of *will*. People with this type of hand express will in the form of primitive outbursts of anger and a great deal of motor activity.

The so-called "reptilian brain" (discussed later) dominates their behavior.

PSYCHOLOGICAL CHARACTERISTICS OF THE ELEMENTARY HAND

The basic demeanor of people with elementary hands is directed towards survival. As long as they have their creature comforts, they are quite happy, and they don't much care about anything else. These people do not always think in a logical manner and they become quite obstinate when faced with something they do not understand.

In a pub I got into conversation with a man who had elementary hands. We chatted for a while and then got round to the subject of politics. After a short time the man became so objectionable that I was forced to change the subject. He had superficial ideas on politics and was quite unamenable to any argument. The only way to continue our conversation was to buy him a beer and chat about less controversial topics.

RELATIONSHIPS

People with elementary hands prefer the purely physical pleasures of life. In relationships, therefore, they attach great importance to the sexual aspect. They are often jealous and can be very possessive about their partners. They also react in a very emotional way if they feel they are being cheated. They would rather give their rival a punch in the jaw than sit down and talk over the problem.

OCCUPATIONS

These people enjoy physical labor, which they prefer to do in the open air. In general, people with elementary hands are not encountered in academic circles or in offices.

HOBBIES

These people are often attracted to combative sports. They are not averse to a bullfight and one of their favorite pastimes is watching boxing or wrestling matches. They themselves are very likely to take part in such sports. They would certainly not read a book about the nature of man, such as this one!

SPIRITUALITY

People with elementary hands believe in one God, as long as that God manifests things to suit them. If things do not turn out as they would wish, however, they promptly lose faith in Him. They are often guided by a blind faith in fortune-tellers, including those who gaze into crystal balls. Superstition seems to be inborn in these people.

Years ago, when I first began doing diagnostic hand analysis, a young man with elementary hands consulted me. In my opinion, I gave him an accurate analysis, which was later confirmed by someone who knew this man well and who had listened to a tape recording of the consultation.

The client, however, found the consultation worthless, basically because I had not seen that his grandmother had recently died. This was in contrast to a woman who had read his future a week earlier. As he had walked in, this woman declared with a dramatic gesture that "death was all around him."

When I asked this client what his grandmother had meant to him, it turned out that she had exercised practically no influence at all on his life. Her death had made little impression on him and could not therefore be read in his hand.

HEALTH

People with these hands have extremely good health. They often possess an iron constitution—unless there is a question of excessive alcohol consumption or exceptionally heavy eating habits.

The Spatulate Hand

PHYSICAL CHARACTERISTICS OF THE SPATULATE HAND

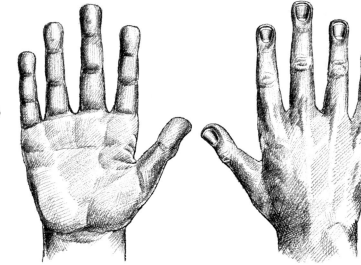

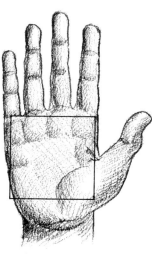

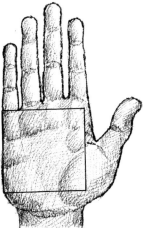

The palm of the hand (see the illustrations in the margin) is either broader at the top than at the bottom or vice versa. We can determine this visually or by drawing a square on the hand itself. If the top is broader, these people are more directed to mental activities. If the bottom is broader, they are more likely to engage in physical activities.

The fingers are spatulate; this means that they are waisted just below the tops (see the illustration).

The palm of the hand is resilient, which indicates a great deal of energy.

The skin texture is "average" and the hands are generally a little hairy.

The thumb is usually long, connoting the motivation to make something out of one's life.

Many lines have formed in the hand, signifying a great deal of activity.

This hand shape particularly indicates the qualities of *love* and *will* (specifically, activity).

PSYCHOLOGICAL CHARACTERISTICS OF THE SPATULATE HAND

Inquiry is the most important motivating factor of people with spatulate hands. They have very broad interests and are particularly curious about anything new. They are therefore extroverted in nature.

They are also particularly communicative. They quickly become enthusiastic and are happy to share their enthusiasm with others. If we want to learn something about these people, or if we want to give them advice, it is also very important to look at the fingers. Hand analysis is a science that takes all facets—thumb, fingers, hand shape, mounts, nails, and lines—into account in order to arrive at the best and most extensive advice possible.

People with a spatulate hand combined with short, smooth fingers, for example, often behave in an impulsive manner. Spatulate palms indicate a great deal of energy and this energy is not restricted by the knuckles.

I remember one young man with such a combination. He came to me in desperation because he did not know what occupation to choose. The choice was, indeed, difficult for him because he jumped from one idea to the next, without ever taking the time to think things through properly.

If people with spatulate palms also have long, knotty fingers, then their excessive spirit of enterprise is held in check by their excessive need for reflection. This combination often results in a tense state of mind because these

Mixed hand shapes

This hand is mainly square but is spatulate at the base. The squareness indicates that behavior is guided by a healthy understanding and a clear view of life. The spatulate shape signifies a delivery of energy when necessary.

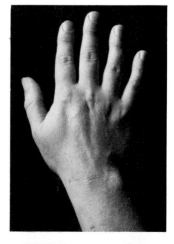

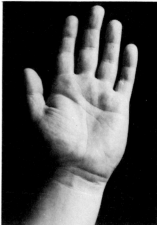

powers work in opposition to each other. These people, however, may make excellent detectives because that profession demands both an inquiring mind and an analytical approach.

In general, people with spatulate hands must learn to use their energy better. If they are unable to coordinate and control their actions, their energy can be wasted in frustrations and aimless activities.

RELATIONSHIPS

Since these people are happy to allow others to share in their enthusiasm, they like to take part in various activities together with their partner. Their capacity for qualitative and quantitative sex is highly valued by partners with the same needs, but less highly valued by partners who are not so warm-blooded. They are certainly not spiteful or resentful; they quickly forget if their partners do them an injustice.

Furthermore, they feel a strong need to express their spirit of enterprise and do not take it kindly when their partners attempt to curtail them.

OCCUPATIONS

People who have palms in which the upper part is broader are usually involved in mental or intellectual investigation. They have, for example, an intense interest in new philosophies (without necessarily harboring a wish to be a philosopher). Journalists often possess spatulate hands, as do many psychologists, therapists, and entrepreneurs, among others.

When the lower part of the palm is broader, then discovery is directed more towards the physical aspects of life. These people might choose, for example, physiotherapy, sculpting, archeology, geology, or biology as occupations.

HOBBIES

These people like to climb mountains or visit historical sites. But if, for one reason or another, they are unable to do these things, then they take great pleasure in visiting a history museum or watching adventure films. They prefer team sports to individual sports because, as stated earlier, they enjoy sharing their enthusiasm with others.

SPIRITUALITY

People with spatulate hands are continually searching for the ultimate truth. This means that they may have a great interest in various esoteric movements. They are strongly motivated to investigate the actual substance of everything that crosses their path. However, this constant desire to investigate can degenerate into restlessness, since it is not always possible to understand the essence of life instantaneously!

These people are often creative and have a desire to spread their creativity to the outside world. The general well-being of humanity is very important to them and they often involve themselves in "good causes."

HEALTH

People with spatulate hands usually enjoy excellent health. Moreover, they often have a healthy appetite because they use so much energy.

The Square Hand

PHYSICAL CHARACTERISTICS OF THE SQUARE HAND

If we look at a square hand, we see immediately that it is, indeed, square—meaning that the palm of the hand is angular and the tops of the fingers seem almost to have been chopped off at right angles.

Mixed hand shapes

Here, the fingers are philosophical, and the fingertips are conic and square. The palm is square and 15 percent spatulate at the base. The spatulate shape connotes physical energy and an inquiring streak. The possessor of this hand bases his decisions on facts, as indicated by the square hand shape, and these decisions are strengthened by his analytical bent, indicated by his philosophical fingers. In this hand, dynamism is coupled with a touch of contemplativeness.

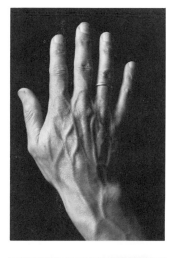

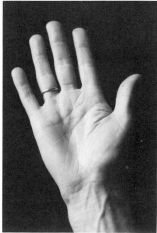

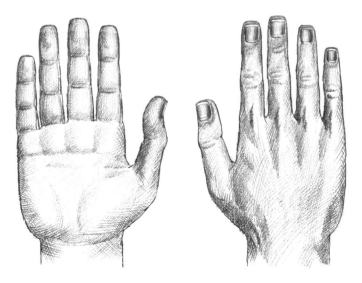

The skin texture is average. The skin looks healthy and radiant; it is a pleasure to touch such a hand.

People with square hands do not usually have flexible fingers. The fingers often have square nails and are usually average in length.

The thumb is long, which again indicates that these people have the motivation to achieve something in life.

The lines in the hand are deep because people with square hands are very intense. This hand shape is particularly associated with the quality of *wisdom*.

PSYCHOLOGICAL CHARACTERISTICS OF THE SQUARE HAND

Of all the "psychological types" delineated by the psychologist C. G. Jung, people with this hand shape correspond most closely to what he called the "extroverted thinking type." In this type of person, objective thinking is the most dominating quality, and such people like to impose order and efficiency on the outside world. In general, people with square hands are orderly, practical, and punctual. They have an intelligent and inquisitive mind, which is chiefly involved with making money and doing business.

Someone with spatulate hands, for example, might

have a social drink in order to have contact with other people, but someone with square hands will follow it up with a business dinner. The saying "time is money" is frequently employed by these people.

They have an open, friendly manner. They are conventional and uninterested in spontaneous frivolity. This is also expressed in the way they dress.

Furthermore, they prefer to be convinced by facts. Vague ideas or revolutionary theories get nowhere with them; they require conclusive evidence.

A striking example of this personality trait was apparent in a businessman who told me that he had laughed uproariously at his wife's intuition about certain transactions. He gradually stopped laughing, however, when this "feminine intuition" proved to be correct. Once her insights took on a practical value for him, he even tried to act on them.

When these people come to me for a consultation, I always have to first convince them of a few facts. Only then do they accept the practical value of diagnostic hand analysis. I think of people with square hands as being the "pillars of society," because they are dependable and reliable and keep the economy running.

RELATIONSHIPS

People with square hands are very trustworthy partners, friends, employers, and employees.

They are honest and straightforward in their dealings and insist on being treated in the same way.

They are excellent breadwinners; their family wants for nothing.

They are not usually romantic and consider that dining by candlelight, for example, is nonsense.

On the sexual level, they are not driven by lust but by pleasure. Therefore, they are creative lovers and take great enjoyment from the pleasure of their partner.

Mixed hand shapes

This hand is a mixture of the conic, square, and spatulate hand shapes. The lower part of the palm is slightly spatulate; the finger of Saturn and the finger of Apollo are spatulate. The fingertips are square and the palm is square and conic.

We can describe this hand as 10 percent spatulate, 45 percent conic, and 45 percent square. The spatulate shape indicates a dynamic approach, the conic a sensitive nature, and the square a practical streak.

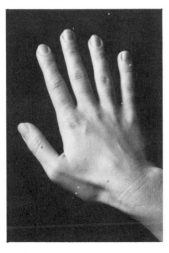

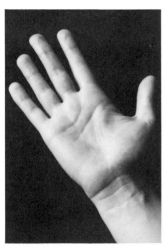

OCCUPATIONS

These people often function very well in occupations that involve practical activities and reasoning. They are thus well-suited as real estate agents, craftspeople, doctors, engineers, teachers, lawyers, businesspeople, or management consultants, for example.

Furthermore, they are very good at building up organizations and management, and they are also found in government circles or in the military. In addition, these people are very efficient at organizing a household.

HOBBIES

Their hobbies are bridge, golf, tennis, hockey, and similar pastimes and sports.

All forms of competition appeal to them and they enjoy watching competitive sports such as baseball. They look for more intellectual recreation at the theater or at a concert.

SPIRITUALITY

They often believe in the divine, as long as their belief can be reasoned. They are most attracted to organized religious services. When the minister or priest is engaged in precise, pragmatic dissertation, people with square hands listen with interest and belief. But if the sermon is too vague, their thoughts tend to return to a more earthly plane.

They are also apt to believe in God as long as He allows business to be profitable. But when setbacks occur, their belief in divine power begins to wane.

They are in no way superstitious and regard "crystal-ball prophecy" as a huge joke.

In addition, they have good powers of concentration and take to meditating, once they are convinced of its value.

HEALTH

People with square hands generally enjoy excellent health.

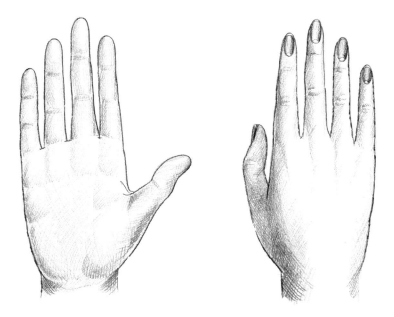

The Conic Hand

PHYSICAL CHARACTERISTICS OF THE CONIC HAND

The palm of the conic hand (see the illustration) is elongated, fleshy, and soft. This indicates a desire for beauty and comfort.

The skin texture is fine and the hand is usually hairless. The skin is pink and smells sweet.

The fingers are long and smooth (without knuckles) and are usually supple enough to be bent back.

The nails are also elongated and usually well cared for.

The thumb of the conic hand is generally of average length.

If we compare the conic hand with the square hand, we see that the conic hand exhibits more "feminine" qualities, such as softness, sensitivity, and powers of imagination. In contrast, the square hand shows signs of more "masculine" qualities, such as power, perseverance, and practically directed intelligence. The conic hand is strongly associated with the quality of *love*.

The universally famous "Mona Lisa" has conic hands.

PSYCHOLOGICAL CHARACTERISTICS OF THE CONIC HAND

People with conic hands are artistic and love everything that is beautiful, pleasurable, and charming. Generally, they have a friendly, gentle nature.

In addition, people with such hands can be vain and very susceptible to flattery.

The longing for comfort and luxury can sometimes gain the upper hand with these people. Because they are not always practical, they sometimes can't achieve this luxury for themselves, and then they may look for other, easier ways to achieve it. Women with conic hands can sometimes be found working for escort agencies and in similar "professions" in which they can earn a great deal of money by "catering" to gentlemen. The conic hand indicates a large measure of intuition. Impressions are received spontaneously and intuitively; therefore, this hand shape is always found in combination with round fingertips.

People with conic hands generally do not possess great perseverance. If they also have short thumbs, then this shortcoming can degenerate into indecisiveness. When this happens, it is very important for the individual to strive for a more resolute and practical attitude towards life.

RELATIONSHIPS

People with conic hands have a great need for love and understanding and they are capable of great affection if they are admired and adored. They express this affection, for example, by furnishing the home in a tasteful manner or by the pleasant way they treat guests.

They are not highly motivated sexually. They are more concerned with feelings of admiration and romance than with the purely physical side of sex.

In one couple I remember, the husband had a square hand and the wife a conic hand. Together, they had a wonderful marriage. He provided the means for her to live in luxury, and she furnished the house with several tasteful art treasures, so enabling him to impress his business associates. Moreover, he complimented her regularly and so she went through life radiantly happy.

OCCUPATIONS

People with conic hands are often found in the artistic professions, which enable them to realize their yearning for beauty. They are often dancers, interior designers, models, beauty specialists, actors, or musicians.

Such people can also be good psychotherapists, because their great intuition gives them the capacity to tune into the psyche of their clients and the roots of their problems.

These people are not usually the first or the best in the exercise of their occupation because, in general, they lack practical and resolute qualities.

Recently I gazed in amazement at a beautifully tended garden. The owner was standing next to me and I gave him my compliments. He then told me that he, too, derived great pleasure from his garden but that he did not maintain it himself. That is a typical characteristic of people with conic hands—they thoroughly enjoy beauty but do not like to get their hands dirty.

HOBBIES

In short, anything that is artistic—from painting to organizing a musical evening—appeals to these people.

SPIRITUALITY

People with conic hands believe in general that there is a creative force in the universe. They are also fascinated by the "unknown" and sometimes try to satisfy their longing for it by attaching themselves to cult groups or to the followers of a guru.

These people can also be superstitious. They are not as superstitious as people with elementary hands, but they are still susceptible.

The best advice such people can be given is to guard against "false prophets."

HEALTH

In general, people with conic hands have a delicate constitution. Their health is also fragile.

They must adopt sensible eating habits and be moderate with alcohol because their body cannot tolerate it very well.

What's more, such people have a tendency to become mentally unstable or neurotic as soon as they sense they are in danger of losing control over their own life.

The Philosophical Hand

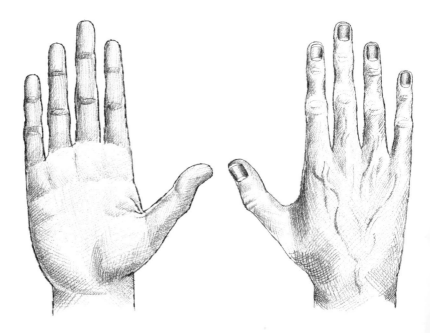

PHYSICAL CHARACTERISTICS OF THE PHILOSOPHICAL HAND

If we look at a philosophical hand (see the illustration), we will almost certainly notice immediately that it appears to be rather bony.

The palm is rectangular in shape.

The fingers are long, thin, and knotty (they have knuckles). The tips of the fingers may be square.

Mostly people with philosophical hands have long thumbs and, in general, are highly disciplined thinkers.

The skin texture is fine and there are usually thick, blue veins running along the back of the hand.

The palm of the hand often shows very deep lines.

This hand is strongly associated with the quality of *wisdom*.

Mixed hand shapes

The palm is 50 percent square and 50 percent conic, and the fingers are philosophic. The unconscious driving force is both artistic and sensitive and yet there is still a feeling for the practical values of life. The philosophical fingers are indicative of sensible and well-considered actions and methods of working.

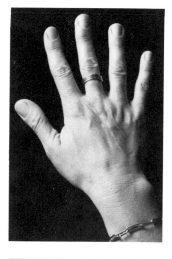

PSYCHOLOGICAL CHARACTERISTICS OF THE PHILOSOPHICAL HAND

People with philosophical hands correspond most closely with Jung's "introverted thinking type." This type has the need to create an inner order. While they are observing facts, their thoughts are directed to their interrelated internal relationships. This type of thinking is deeper and more theoretical than the type of thinking of, say, square-handed people, whose thinking is more superficial and moves from one idea to the next.

People with philosophical hands are drawn towards an intellectual approach to life. Therefore, they attach little value to the intuitive inclination of, for example, people with conic hands. Neither are they particularly impressed by the businesslike approach of, among others, square-handed people.

A person with this hand shape is, in essence, a scientific or philosophic theorist, the type who is forever examining basic assumptions or formulating new abstractions to account for observations. They are sometimes real "egg-heads," tend to prefer their own company, and, in con-

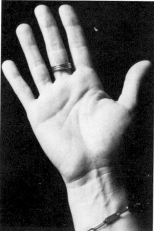

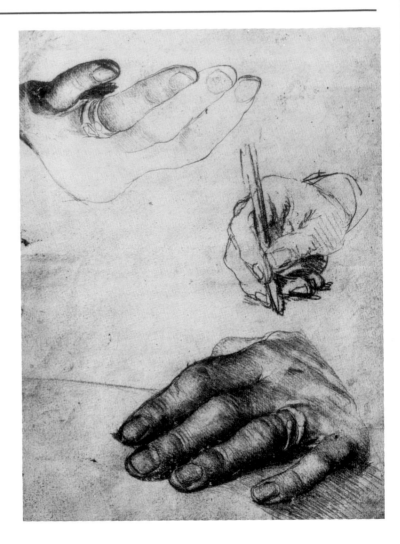

The hands of Desiderius Erasmus, the Dutch philosopher, drawn by Holbein.

trast to spatulate-handed people, show little interest in the outside world.

With the aid of books on philosophy and philosophical discussions, they attempt to discover what life is really all about. This intellectual search for suppositions is a very different process than that of reaching conclusions about the reality of life by means of intuitive receptivity.

People with philosophical hands seek the certainty of proof and their mind is at peace as long as such proof can be found. But as soon as the proof seems to be inconclusive, they immediately begin a restless search for further proofs.

Often these people can behave in an intellectually proud

and inflexible manner. After a great deal of thought, they have developed a particular intellectual philosophy, which, in their eyes, is the "only real truth," and it is extremely difficult to shift them from it.

RELATIONSHIPS

Initially, these people do not look for emotional intimacy and physical closeness in a relationship. On the contrary, they look for a relationship that stimulates them intellectually. If that intellectual contact is not present, it is difficult for them to make physical contact.

I can remember a mathematics teacher who delighted in writing completely incomprehensible notations on the blackboard for a complete period. Very few students had any idea what it was all about, but he himself enjoyed every moment of the class. Fortunately, he was married to a most caring woman who made sure he ate regularly and remembered to change his socks. He was so involved in intellectual reflection that without her he would have forgotten to attend to these mundane things!

Another example: Beethoven lived in a squalor of unwashed dishes and other garbage. He had evidently become so intellectually engrossed in his music that he was no longer aware of everyday life around him.

OCCUPATIONS

People with philosophical hands are almost always found in occupations that stimulate their inquiring mind. They might be teachers, writers of scientific books, judges, psychologists, psychoanalysts, professors, and the like. Or they may be engaged in developing new forms of government or new theories to aid technological advancement.

Even a grocer with this hand shape cannot escape his nature and will attempt to explain the economic and political state of the world while slicing the ham for his customers.

HOBBIES

Their greatest joy in life is to sit in their study reading. They also enjoy listening to classical music and can usually be persuaded to play a game of chess.

SPIRITUALITY

People with philosophical hands endeavor to use their intellect to understand the spiritual. They inquire into the mysteries of life and believe that they can only develop their consciousness by thinking. They are able, for example, to "think out" a new religion. Calvin is a striking example of such a person.

A piece of good advice for these intellectually oriented people is for them to be a little more receptive to a sense of spirituality that comes from the heart.

HEALTH

As already mentioned, these people are so busy with their intellectual contemplations that they tend to neglect their eating and sleeping habits.

The Psychic Hand

PHYSICAL CHARACTERISTICS OF THE PSYCHIC HAND

Psychic hands (see the illustration on the opposite page) are long and thin, and generally appear beautiful and gracious.

The fingers are pointed and are not usually knotty.

The color varies from pink to white. Sometimes it even appears as if the hand is translucent.

The skin texture is very refined and the hand contains very fine lines.

The thumb is usually short.

This hand is most closely related to the quality of *love*.

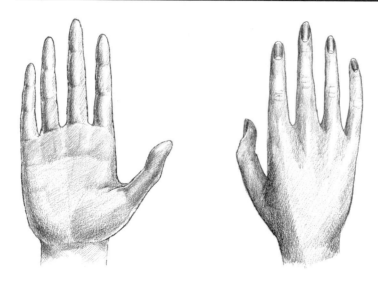

PSYCHOLOGICAL CHARACTERISTICS OF THE PSYCHIC HAND

People with this type of hand can be most closely compared with Jung's "introverted intuitive type." Jung stated that a lack of practical sense was the main characteristic of this type of person.

People with psychic hands are extremely idealistic—in fact, they are so idealistic that they can sometimes appear rather unworldly. They tend to be dreamers and to arrive at their opinions intuitively, often without the intermediary of thought. Thus, they find it difficult to reason out their views to others.

Someone with philosophical hands, for example, would probably be driven mad by someone with psychic hands. This is because philosophical people wish to confirm every viewpoint with firm evidence and psychic people find it very hard to explain their subtle impressions from other planes of consciousness. On the other hand, psychic people are often very irritated by the long-winded explanations of philosophical people, because they feel that their intuitive "knowing" is beyond debate.

Although it is important for people with psychic hands to further develop their intuition, which would enable them to give others excellent advice, they still must attempt to keep both feet on the ground. They should try to combine their gifts of intuition with the reality of everyday life.

I once met someone with psychic hands who told me that unpleasant things would happen in his life—he felt it. I believed him and asked him what he was going to do about it. He said he had not got round to thinking about that!

People with psychic hands have a tendency to keep their head in the clouds and rely on invisible friends rather than trying to find the solution to a problem themselves.

RELATIONSHIPS

The relationships of people with psychic hands are not always stable. They can become fascinated by someone, but this fascination does not usually last very long. They may even enter into marriage on the basis of an idealistic fascination rather than on the basis of more firmly grounded, practical considerations. They want to be free and not hindered in their self-expression. They need sympathetic and tolerant partners who allow them the freedom to function in their own way. They are not particularly interested in purely physical relationships, but tend to seek contacts in spiritual movements and the company of like-minded people.

OCCUPATIONS

These people prefer to have work in which they can be fully true to themselves and during which they are not faced with limitations or confronted with high expectations. They therefore work best in a quiet, relaxed environment. Because they are not particularly materialistic, they do not usually make successful businesspeople.

Technical or organizational work does not interest them at all.

They can, however, make excellent clairvoyants or psychotherapists, if they can learn to harness and control their intuitive gifts.

The last time I walked into a local health food shop, I noticed that the owner had psychic hands. She talked knowledgeably and devotedly about all the products and their "cosmic" background, but her administration of the shop—I found out later—was in total chaos.

HOBBIES

People with psychic hands often enjoy walking through the countryside and like close contact with nature. Among other things, they enjoy Gregorian and "New Age" music and often meditate. Furthermore, they communicate frequently with their "invisible helpers."

SPIRITUALITY

In terms of their spirituality, they can have extreme devotion to their internal master and helpers. This can be seen in contrast to people with conic hands who often revere an external master, such as a guru. Furthermore, these people sometimes have precognitive abilities.

Some time ago in my practice I was consulted by a man with psychic hands. He was most surprised that I could immediately ascertain his problems and then offer him advice. He was well able to help others, but could not help himself.

HEALTH

In general, people with psychic hands have delicate health. Their nervous system must be strengthened by healthy eating and perhaps massage. In addition, they often have weak lungs and are susceptible to colds, influenza, bronchitis, and pneumonia. These ailments are caused by the transfer of their oversensitive feelings to their lungs.

6·MOUNTS AND FINGERS

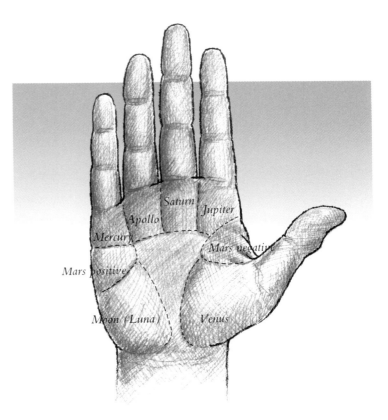

Saturn
Apollo
Jupiter
Mercury
Mars negative
Mars positive
Moon (Luna)
Venus

The mounts in our hands are most closely associated with our general behavior. As explained in the previous chapters, the thumb symbolizes the motivation of an individual to apply the three primary qualities of *will, wisdom,* and *love* in life, and the different hand shapes represent the basic character of the individual. The mounts reflect the details of that basic character—in other words, our individual qualities.

Let us compare our hand to a tree. The roots can be seen as symbolizing the thumb; the trunk, the shape of the hand; and the branches, the mounts. As the branches of a tree bear fruit, so the mounts "bear" our cultivated or neglected qualities, and indicate our capacity to lead a fruitful life.

The mounts (see the illustration) are the balls, or pads, of flesh that bulge up from the palm and their names are taken from Roman mythology.

The mounts also symbolize the archetype of man. Archetypes are the primeval content of the collective unconscious, consisting of inherited ideas and predispositions. Each archetype—also known as planetary type or *manvantara* (planetary-spiritual power)—represents an unconscious pattern of physical, emotional, and intellectual behavior and also reflects a particular physical appearance. Since Roman times, artists have expressed these mythological forms of appearance in statues and paintings. There are seven planetary types and the physique of every person is shaped according to one or more of them. The mounts, or archetypes, create, as it were, "subpersonalities," which together form the complete personality.

The mounts in our hand and the fingers are dependent on one another, which is perhaps best illustrated by a detail from a painting called "No Man Is an Island unto Himself (John Donne)." As human beings, we are all, to some extent, dependent on one another.

Detail from the painting "No Man Is an Island unto Himself (John Donne)."

We can draw an analogy here from our own life. When, for example, one partner makes a decision, that decision influences the life of the other partner. In the same way, mounts form a pattern of action and reaction.

I will now describe briefly the different qualities of the various mounts.

Evolutionary hand analysis (see the illustration) is carried out counterclockwise. This is because the earth on which we live is a planet of opposition and we can only learn if we experience opposition.

Conception is found in the mount named Luna (commonly called the Mount of Moon). If we follow the process of birth and development, then the child or the idea is born in Luna. Problems in the reproductive organs of women can often be read in the Mount of Moon.

The child or the idea takes form in Venus. We want to

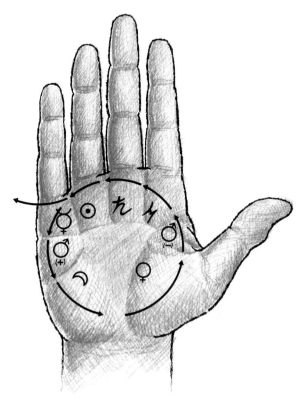

manifest in life, so we must adopt a certain stance. This is also true of an idea—if we want to put it into practice, we must give it a particular form.

An architect, for example, has an idea for a building. He sets out this idea in the form of a drawing on paper. The design then takes physical shape through its construction.

In the Mount of Mars negative we find the strength and the powers of speech needed to achieve things in life and to put our ideas into practice. This mount therefore represents our physical energy.

The Mount of Jupiter gives us our means of identification—our ego sense. This self-awareness enables us to hold our own in life. The Mount of Jupiter gives us the capacity to weld together, as it were, the ideas and thoughts of Luna and Venus. In short, through Jupiter we learn to form patterns of thought.

The Mount of Saturn provides the opportunity to broaden that thinking. Because of this, man has the ability to "turn inside himself and seek contact with his soul." The quality of thinking from Jupiter takes depth in Saturn.

In Apollo (the sun) we learn how to face the outside world. This mount gives us the energy, the cheerfulness, and the optimism to cope with life, to serve others lovingly, and to share our ideas with them.

The Mount of Mercury gives us the capacity to remember and to coordinate. It also gives us the desire to be involved with other people and in the activities of the world at large.

According to Eastern philosophies, one of the paradoxes of life is that we must first become completely involved in life, in order to learn and grow from its experiences, before we can set ourselves free of our attachment to possessions, to other people, and even to our earthly life. Detachment is necessary in order to reach *moksha,* ultimate liberation, and *nirvana,* oneness with the divine.

This urge for detachment is also established in Mercury. The Italian artist Giovanni da Bologna (1506) showed this

Mercury

most strikingly in his sculpture of the god Mercury, who almost seems to be escaping the force of gravity.

The Mount of Mars positive represents our mental strength and also our ability to remember. This faculty of memory, however, is rather more emotionally "colored" than that of Mercury. Here, almost all our thinking is based on subjective conscious or unconscious memories. Mars positive registers, as it were, whether what we have encountered in this life or in previous lives has been experienced in a positive or a negative way. If we are carrying many positive memories with us, then our mental outlook is optimistic. In contrast, if we are carrying many negative memories, our mental outlook is pessimistic and we do not have high expectations in life.

The Meaning of Underdeveloped and Overdeveloped Mounts

As we have already seen, mounts represent our individual qualities. These mounts (and the qualities they represent) can be well-developed, underdeveloped, or overdeveloped. This same principle operates with the thumb and fingers.

The qualities indicated by a mount are at their best when that mount is well-developed. If the mount is underdeveloped (flat or even concave), then the qualities of this mount are not sufficiently developed. If the mount is overdeveloped (exceptionally rounded), then we are putting too much energy behind the qualities of this mount as we put them into practice.

Before discussing the mounts in further detail, I would like to explain how The Tale of Snow White and the Seven Dwarfs, *written by the brothers Grimm and later made into a film by Walt Disney, helps us better understand the meaning of the mounts.*

The wicked stepmother represents "evil" and Snow White

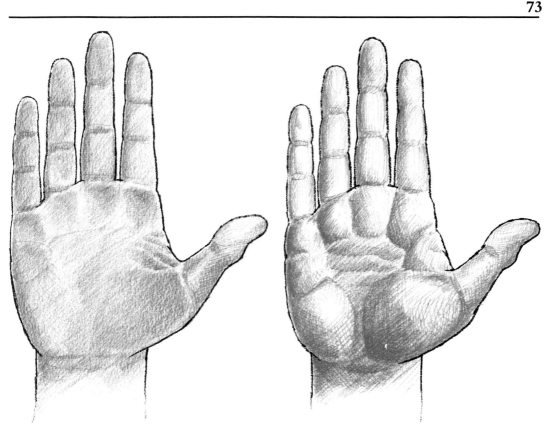

Underdeveloped mounts   Overdeveloped mounts

represents "the soul" or "good." The mounts reflect the presence of these forces in man.

The stepmother (evil) was responsible for driving Snow White (the soul) out of paradise (represented in the fairy tale by the palace). Snow White is forced to find her own way through the forest, as we must find our way through life. Eventually she goes to live in a house (the body) with seven dwarfs (the seven mounts). Snow White remains in the house (the body) and day by day, through diligent labor and experience, the dwarfs learn the lessons of life—lessons that Snow White (the young soul) must bring to maturity.

Each of the dwarfs possesses specific qualities of character and physical form. Doc, for example, behaves in a rather pompous manner, though it does not do him much good. He is the leader of the group, nonetheless. The dwarf Happy is very boastful. But he is always telling jokes, has a high-pitched giggling laugh, and is rather corpulent. In short, just like the seven mounts (or *archetypes), these seven dwarfs contain both virtue and vice and they represent all the qualities that we manifest ourselves.*

The wicked stepmother travels over the seven hills (again, the seven mounts) to the house of Snow White and the seven dwarfs and succeeds in tempting Snow White (the soul) to eat the poisoned apple. Snow White's eagerness to taste the apple reveals her vulnerability to temptation—a "vice" that is present in every human being. Because she is ignorant of the consequences of what she has done, Snow White does not die but falls into a deep sleep. Not without reason did Plato call life "the sleep of ignorance."

The dwarfs dig for ore, searching especially for gold. Through their exertions, they are symbolically striving to achieve perfection—just like the planetary types. Aristotle declared many centuries ago that everything in nature strives for perfection. Gold is the purest metal and a symbol of light.

The dwarfs were not spared their grief over Snow White. In our lives, it is much the same. We learn the lessons of life through hard work and suffering. No one can escape that. The lessons we must learn, how well we learn them, and the manner in which we apply what we have learned, can mainly be read from the mounts of the hand.

In various spiritual traditions, man is regarded as a creature of divine origin who will return again to the divine state if he achieves spiritual maturity through exertion, suffering, and joy. The prince who kisses Snow White (the soul) awake represents the divine power that brings the soul, now fully matured and purified by suffering, back to its divine origins. There, together, they "live happily ever after."

Goethe described this process superbly with the words "Wer nie sein Brot mit Tränen ass, wer nie die kummervollen Nächte auf seinem Bette weinend sass, der kennt euch nicht, ihr himmlische Mächte." Roughly translated this means: "He who never ate with tears his bread, he who never in the troubled night lay weeping in his bed, he knows you not, or heavenly might."

The Mount of Moon (Luna)

LUNA: The Goddess of the Hunt and Unmarried Maidens, the Twin Sister of Apollo

Luna (see the illustration) is the mount that is most indicative of our senses. All the senses are filtered, as it were, through Luna. We receive the outside world through this mount. We also reveal ourselves through Luna. The Mount of Moon indicates the manner, or attitude, in which we relate to the outside world.

In general, Lunarians are charming people. They are—both men and women—caring and cared for. Positive Lunarians are receptive to the feelings of other people and they respond with common sense to the world around them.

Luna is most closely associated with the quality of *love*.

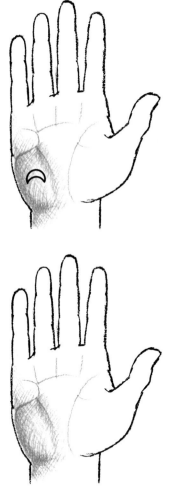

WELL-DEVELOPED LUNA

Key words: imagination
                receptivity
                conceptual creativity

A well-developed Mount of Moon (see the illustration) indicates a healthy imagination. These people are also exceptionally receptive to impressions from the environment and from other people.

A well-developed mount also means—as is the case with the thumb and fingers—that there is a strong harmony between the qualities of the mount and the manner in which they are applied in everyday life.

UNDERDEVELOPED LUNA

Key words: suspicion
　　　　　　tactlessness
　　　　　　fear of rejection

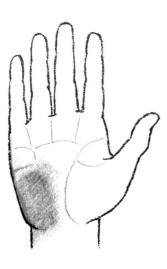

An underdeveloped, or flat, Mount of Moon (see the illustration) connotes an inability to receive the world. These people attempt to shut out the world and are not receptive to others.

Although they do possess the senses to do so, they do not absorb impressions. These people are afraid of rejection and so in turn they react by rejecting the world. In this way, they find themselves in a vicious circle. If we shut out the world, then sooner or later the world will shut us out.

A striking description of this situation is given in "The Dialogue" from the Book of Job in the Old Testament of the Bible: "Whatever I fear comes true, whatever I dread befalls me." This means that we often attract the very things of which we are afraid. Therefore, if we fear rejection, that is what we get.

People with an underdeveloped Luna move heaven and earth to avoid pain and, as said of the ostrich, they bury their head in the sand. Ironically, they are faced with pain simply because they have not protected themselves adequately against it. If we refuse to allow other people to get close to us, we can never sense when someone is about to hurt us. As long as we do not know what to expect, we remain suspicious. Or we may act in a blindly impulsive and tactless manner, which in turn can make us nervous and afraid.

People with an underdeveloped Luna must try to open their senses more to the world so that they can enjoy life more fully.

OVERDEVELOPED LUNA

Key words: hypocrisy
flattery
hallucinations

People with an overdeveloped, rounded Mount of Moon (see the illustration) usually have difficulty keeping their creativity under control, and when this happens, their creativity can degenerate into unbridled fantasy. These people are insecure because they cannot find themselves. The moon reflects the light of the sun and they seek the light outside themselves. If the influence of the Moon is too strong, they attempt to capture the light of others. They begin to imitate other people and often engage in role playing. This is a perfect quality for actors, but it does not provide a good basis for everyday life.

These people are also afraid that they will not be accepted by others. This fear can lead to flattery and hypocrisy as they try to get in people's good graces. They also employ drama and self-pity in their attempts to achieve this end.

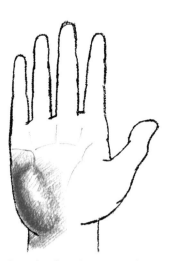

Overdeveloped Mount of Moon

Men with an overdeveloped Mount of Moon often have a strong mother fixation. They frequently see their wife as a mother figure—which is not always appreciated by their wife.

People with an extremely highly developed Mount of Moon (see the illustration) are often inclined to betray the trust of others. They commit crimes with great charm and ingenuity. If we read an article in the newspaper about a charming gentleman who makes it a habit of relieving lonely widows of their savings, we can be fairly sure that he has an overdeveloped Mount of Moon.

These people should learn that honesty is the best policy. Men with such a mount often possess great powers of sensual attraction and women with this mount are often flirtatious.

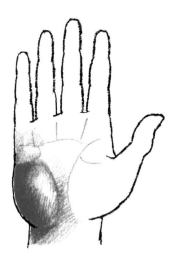

Very overdeveloped Mount of Moon

The Mount of Venus

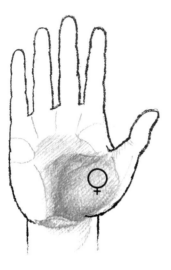

VENUS: Goddess of Love

Indications that have to do with forming or shaping are found in the Mount of Venus (see the illustration). Venus not only gives form to "the child," but also, for example, to ideas, art, a house, a family, and a business. The feelings of Venus have the potential to be expressed in pure creativity. This is in contrast to Luna, which, as it is more closely connected with the five senses, remains on a more emotional level.

The Mount of Venus is particularly associated with the quality of *love*.

The word "emotion" is derived from the Latin word "exmovere." "Ex" means "out" and "movere" means "to move." Emotions must be expressed (come out) and this expression stirs (moves) us to action. An emotion is the reaction to an event. For example, if we lash out at someone in the heat of a bitter argument, we get rid of our emotion and it doesn't bother us anymore.

Animals behave instinctively, but human beings have been blessed with intelligence. We think first and "process" an event through our feelings before we act. In this way, our actions are delayed, and delayed actions mean tension. In human beings, this is often the root cause of stress.

Emotional, or inner, life is found in Venus whereas the source of emotional reactions is found in Luna. The philosopher Spinoza stated that all knowledge is "affective knowledge" received through the senses (Luna) and processed mentally (Jupiter) and through feelings (Venus). He described this digested knowledge as "pure knowledge," which is reproduced as "intuition."

Intuition is a feeling that is established in Venus. The Mount of Venus therefore contains signs that point to an "intuitive power of discernment."

Lunarians receive ideas and Venusians can say whether an idea is good or bad.

The Mount of Venus also contains many signs that are indicative of the major concerns of Plato and other philosophers—namely, truth, goodness, and beauty. If we possess these attributes, pure love is created.

Love is the cradle of our ability to feel. Venus gives us receptivity (the ability to receive and give love), by which we give meaning and intimacy to relationships. True Venusians much prefer to live in harmony.

WELL-DEVELOPED MOUNT OF VENUS

Key words: truth
                goodness
                beauty

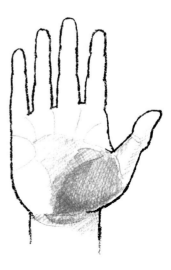

In people with a well-developed Mount of Venus (see the illustration), the three qualities of truth, goodness, and beauty are in balance.

If we now examine the thumb again, we can discover if all three phalanges are in balance. The third phalanx of the thumb is the Mount of Venus.

People with a well-developed Mount of Venus have the capacity to both receive and give love. By this is meant all the various types of love—such as, sexual love, the love of a friend, and the love of God. Venusians are usually heartwarming people who genuinely enjoy life, and this enjoyment binds them pleasurably to other people and to their environment. Venusians create pleasure for those around them and enjoy establishing a cozy, colorful, and tasteful atmosphere in the home.

UNDERDEVELOPED MOUNT OF VENUS

Key words: passivity
                listlessness
                indifference to love

Venusians attach great value to harmony, but if they do not experience it they may soon give up the struggle. If the Mount of Venus is underdeveloped (see the illustra-

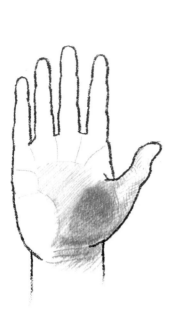

tion), these people have little motivation (shown in the thumb) to enjoy life.

Many motor nerves are found under the Mount of Venus, and when it is underdeveloped (the mount is flat), they are cramped. The Mount of Venus is bound to the heart and to love, and neither can be activated when the nerves are cramped; love requires energy.

This results in listlessness and indifference. Love is a feeling and a desire, and without desire we become bogged down in passive behavior. Passivity is the opposite pole from love.

If this listless feeling has not completely taken over, people with a flat Mount of Venus sometimes seek love through intermediaries such as a guru. They have a strong longing for love but seek these higher feelings outside themselves. There's nothing wrong with following a guru, but eventually these people must find the guru within themselves.

OVERDEVELOPED MOUNT OF VENUS

Key words: avariciousness
     voluptuousness
     coarse life-style

We can say that the coarser the Mount of Venus is, the greater the indications are for a lack of pure love and refinement.

People with a very high Mount of Venus (see the illustration) are therefore mainly interested in their own pleasure—and not in that of others. They tend to be materialistic and avaricious.

The love of these people is directed to the body as opposed to the soul, and the arts of seduction come easily to them.

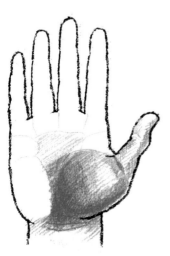

I have known artists with on overdeveloped Mount of Venus who regarded art not as a means of enriching the soul but as a means of enriching their bank accounts. It is also likely that pimps have such an overdeveloped mount.

The Mount of Mars Negative

MARS: God of War

As we have seen earlier, Mars negative (see the illustration) represents physical power. This energy flows out of our internal source and enables us to manifest ourselves in life. Mars negative tells something about our experience and self-expression. From this mount, we can discover whether a person performs in a normal, a self-effacing, or an exaggerated manner.

The word "negative" in the name of the mount does not, however, suggest negative qualities. Mars has two poles: a physical pole and a mental. Mars negative represents physical energy and Mars positive mental energy. We can compare these energies with electricity, which only functions by means of positive and negative currents.

Mars negative is most closely associated with the quality of *will*.

WELL-DEVELOPED MOUNT OF MARS NEGATIVE

Key words: enthusiasm
             sportsmanship
             physical strength

The physical energy of people with a well-developed Mount of Mars negative is usually expressed in the more material fields and the accomplishments of such people are therefore tangible.

They approach everything with enthusiasm. They are fond of sports and possess a healthy urge to manifest in life. They therefore have the personal power to be what they are. They exhibit a healthy self-esteem and self-love without setting themselves above or below other people.

Women with a well-developed Mount of Mars negative, for example, make keen mothers who—in a healthy manner—keep their children under their wings.

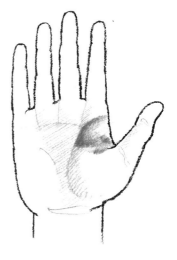

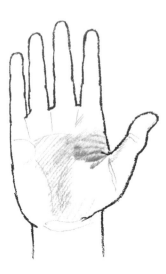

UNDERDEVELOPED MOUNT OF MARS NEGATIVE

Key words: helplessness
low self-esteem
lack of determination

An underdeveloped Mount of Mars negative (see the illustration) indicates a lack of dynamism. People with such a flat mount are generally low-spirited and lack assertiveness. Because they do not stand up for themselves enough, this often means that they do not have sufficient self-esteem. These people feel insecure, tend to avoid confrontations, and often play a helpless role. Servile, self-effacing, and compliant behavior is a hallmark of these people. They must learn to realize that healthy self-esteem and self-love are essential traits to develop.

Sometimes in my practice I see people whose Mount of Mars negative is rather flat only on the side nearer the thumb. As children these people lacked self-esteem and self-confidence. However, over the course of time both their self-esteem and their confidence grew, and their Mount of Mars negative became thicker on the inside. This points to an increasing self-respect.

I also see frequently that this mount becomes weaker and flatter as people become older. This indicates that their vitality is ebbing away slowly.

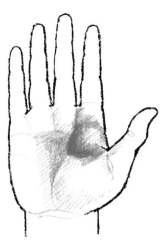

OVERDEVELOPED MOUNT OF MARS NEGATIVE

Key words: fiery temperament
aggressiveness
sarcasm

If the Mount of Mars negative is highly overdeveloped (see the illustration), then the inherent power can degenerate into rage. People with such a mount are almost untameable. They enjoy exercising power over others, but if they cannot immediately attain this power they become inflamed. And if somebody with an overdeveloped Mars negative becomes inflamed, then all hell can break loose!

People with this mount also express their anger verbally, in abusive language or biting sarcasm. Due to their aggressive behavior and their desire to exercise power over others, these people often push others away. Deep in their heart they want to be friendly and so they react to this rejection with sarcasm. They have not yet realized, however, that the rejection is the result of their own behavior.

They must restructure their need for power over others into a power to approach or assist others in a normal manner. People with an overdeveloped Mount of Mars negative often makes excellent managers who happily work to build up an organization, thus satisfying their desire for power. A large percentage of all activities in this world are, in essence, brought about by neurotic behavioral patterns.

I have met men with an overdeveloped Mount of Mars negative who voluntarily joined commando units in the Second War War and the Korean War. It was clear that these people were indulging their aggressiveness in this way.

The Mount and Finger of Jupiter

JUPITER: God of the Gods

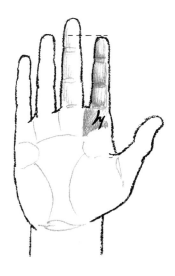

The Mount of Jupiter (see the illustration) is concerned with our identification. Whereas the Mount of Mars negative deals with out physical expression, the Mount of Jupiter focuses on our personality. Therefore, Mars negative is indicative of our power to perform physically and Jupiter is indicative of our power to perform mentally.

True Jupiterians are often leaders in our society in political and economic as well as religious fields. This is not particularly remarkable, as Jupiter is the god of gods.

Identification and leadership can also signify competition. Competition in itself involves testing ourselves against the competence of others. If we are actually ourselves, we are aware of our competence. We can "flow" and this produces a feeling of balance. But if we decide intellectually who we are (or are not), we no longer flow, and we tend to assert ourselves by playing a particular role.

Freud called this phenomenon the "superego," or the "ego ideal," which is formed through identification with norms imposed in youth primarily by parents, teachers, or clergymen, and in later life by, for example, codes of behavior associated with a particular profession. In other words, norms imposed externally have created a pseudo self that compels us to play a certain role. This "superego" can be found in Jupiter.

The Mount of Jupiter is also indicative of our being able to eventually return to our divine origins, or the source. With the help of this mount, we are able to overcome the meaner side of our nature. It is for this reason that we have received our individual consciousness and intelligence. In general, it can be said that a pure Jupiterian is a fine and noble person. Jupiter is most closely associated with the quality of *wisdom.*

The Mount of Jupiter is the first mount that has a finger—the finger of Jupiter. In the mounts of Moon, Venus, and Mars negative and positive, the development of the mount itself is of importance. However, in Jupiter (and also Saturn, Apollo, and Mercury), it is the length of the finger of the mount—whether it is of normal length, or long or short—that is of most importance.

We measure the finger of Jupiter (see the illustration) by laying it beside the finger of Saturn (the middle finger). We draw a line across the middle of the first phalanx of this finger. If the tip of the finger of Jupiter reaches this line exactly, then the finger is of normal length. If the tip of the finger is above this line, the finger is long; if the tip is below the line, the finger is short.

The length of the finger of Jupiter must be measured

exactly because a millimetre or two either way can have great significance regarding behavior.

As mentioned before, the palm of the hand is indicative of unconscious energy. Since the mounts are part of the palm, they also represent our unconscious energy. The qualities stored in the palm are expressed externally, as it were, by the fingers. In other words, the fingers radiate conscious energy and put (to a greater or lesser extent) these stored qualities into practice. Whether a finger is of normal length, or is long or short, is of great importance in the utilization of this energy.

WELL-DEVELOPED FINGER OF JUPITER

Key words: leadership
          compassion
          joviality

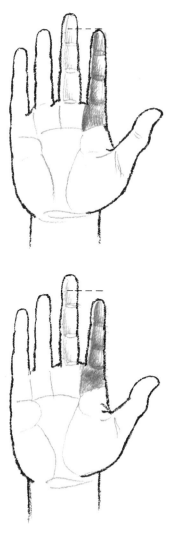

Jupiter is concerned with our ego identification. Such identification can also lead to ambition. People with a well-developed (or normal-length) finger of Jupiter (see the illustration) possess a healthy form of ambition. Goethe put this strikingly with the words "Do not be ambitious, but live as if you would be ambitious." Jupiter also gives direction to our intellect. People with such a finger are in an excellent position to lead and to teach other people—and are happy to do so. They also have a great interest in culture and often have a religious or spiritual streak.

Jupiter is bound to the frontal lobe of our brain and gives us the capacity for abstract thinking.

UNDERDEVELOPED FINGER OF JUPITER

Key words: procrastination
          fear of failure
          lack of self-confidence

People with an underdeveloped, or short, finger of Jupiter (see the illustration) are afraid that they will not be successful in life. The full capacities of the Mount of Jupiter cannot be developed and this promotes a feeling of insecurity. These people develop a fear of failure and have an inferiority complex.

A person with a large inferiority complex sometimes attempts to hide it by telling lies, or his uncertainty and fear may make him afraid to act. He is continually putting things off, although he always has a "rational" explanation

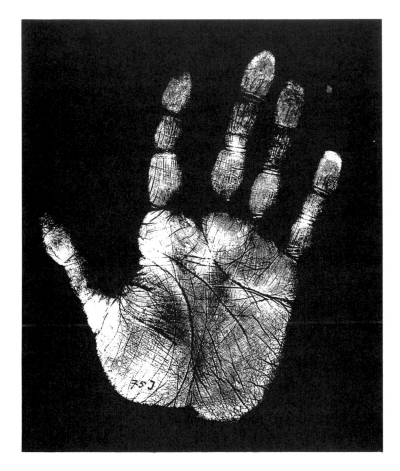

Print of Jung's right hand

for doing so. Such people also find it difficult to make decisions because they lack a sense of direction in their life. Moreover, they don't like making decisions because decisions usually concern the future. If someone is afraid of achievement, then he is also afraid of the future.

I know from experience that people with an underdeveloped finger of Jupiter have a continual tendency to prove themselves. I have also observed that his urge to prove themselves can be so strong that these people no longer recognize their own limitations. This urge can spur them on to great achievements, yet at the same time they remain awkward and obstructive.

Carl Gustav Jung had short fingers of Jupiter and, of course, there is no need to expand on his achievements. Yet he was still obstructive with regard to his mentor Freud.

Krishnamurti, one of the most popular spiritual teachers, also had short fingers of Jupiter, yet he contributed greatly to the spiritual development of many people. However, Krishnamurti also proved to be obstructive when he distanced himself from the Theosophical Movement.

The lives of Jung and Krishnamurti prove that the human soul is often strong enough to overcome the limitations of the personality. Many successful businesspeople have similar short fingers of Jupiter and the urge to prove themselves spurs them on to great achievements. Once these people have reached the goals they have set themselves, this urge to achieve transforms into self-confidence.

Jupiter

People with an underdeveloped finger of Jupiter feel frustrations deeply and, because of their behavior, can often be frustrating to others. However, optimism and an affectionate tolerance can work wonders with such people.

Overdeveloped Finger of Jupiter

Key words: egoism
　　　　　arrogance
　　　　　fanaticism

People with an overdeveloped, or long, finger of Jupiter (see the illustration) are often proud and possess a strongly developed superego. This "ego ideal" is a powerful taskmaster both for themselves and for others.

The power that Jupiter radiates through the finger is

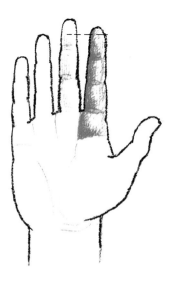

frequently used to impose doctrines on other people. Just as people with an overdeveloped Mars negative wish to exercise physical power over others, these people attempt to attain mental power over others. Their religious or spiritual leaning now becomes dogma. We have seen this trait in certain television evangelists, who, with their finger of Jupiter pointing to Heaven, tell their followers what they must believe and how they must behave, while they themselves frequently misbehave! Such misbehavior was not foreign to the god Jupiter, who was known to be fond of women, both mortal and immortal!

People with an overdeveloped finger of Jupiter are actually too individualistic and often place themselves above other people.

They may also have strong judgments as to how their fellow man should behave and are quick to condemn others if they do not live up to their standards.

Sometimes they are able to cleverly manipulate others by arousing feelings of guilt within them.

Their capacity for abstract thinking can lead to a fearful attitude towards the future. These people must therefore learn to live in the present rather than attempting to safeguard the future. They have a tendency to suppress their feelings and try to control matters intellectually instead. Therefore, they are also restless people. Franklin D. Roosevelt's phrase "The only thing we have to fear is fear itself" applies to these people.

The Mount and Finger of Saturn

SATURN: God of Time (Chronos)

As briefly mentioned at the beginning of this chapter, Saturn (see the illustration) has to do with our thinking. True Saturnians are inclined to reason things out, and this includes both spiritual and material matters. They happily shut themselves away in their study and become immersed in a thorough step-by-step analysis and proof of various subjects.

In Greek mythology, Saturn is known as "Chronos," which means "time." The thoughts of Saturnians therefore tend to be bound to time and directed towards worldly matters. These people also feel attracted to the products of the earth. Therefore, they function extremely well in scientific and agricultural occupations and in those related to the science of physics. Saturn is especially associated with the quality of *wisdom*.

I will now describe the physical appearance of one planet type in order to give you an idea of how planet types look. I have chosen Saturn because the influences of the mount and finger of Saturn are the most difficult to see in relation to the other mounts and fingers.

THE SATURN TYPE

Saturn is the tallest of all the types. The body is thin and bony, the shoulders are stooped, and the skin shows blue veins.

Skin:	Yellow, rough, dry, and wrinkled.
Head:	Long face, high cheekbones, hollow cheeks.
Hair:	Coarse, and in men a tendency to baldness on top of the skull.
Eyebrows:	Bristly eyebrows that grow together at the bridge of the nose and curl upwards at the outer ends.
Ears:	Large ears that stand out from the head.
Teeth:	Long, large teeth wtih dark-colored gums.
Chin:	Thin, pointed chin; men sometimes have a pointed beard.
Nose:	Long, sometimes curved nose, pointed at the end.
Eyes:	Deep-set; somber, sad gaze; melancholic; rings under the eyes.
Mouth:	Large, with thin lips that are dry, rough, and irregularly shaped.

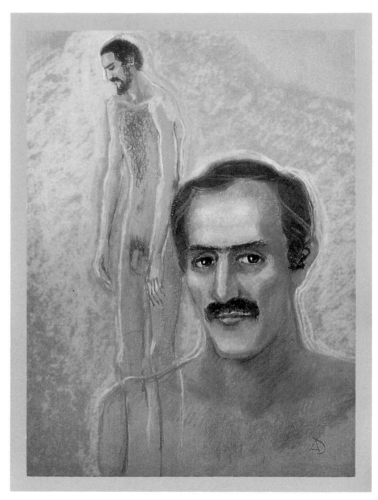

The Saturn type

Upper body:	Prominent Adam's apple and long, thin neck. High, drooping shoulders. Long arms that hang in a lifeless manner at the sides. Flat stomach. Thin chest and cramped lungs. Women have small breasts.
Lower body:	Deep-lying navel. Narrow hips and thighs. Prominent knees. Narrow, long feet and large toes.
Walk:	Shuffling, listless gait.
Voice:	Monotonous, harsh.
Sexual organs:	In men, long and thin, blue-veined. In women, long, deep and narrow.

How to measure the finger of Saturn was described in the chapter on fingers and nails, but for the sake of simplicity I will repeat the procedure here.

Lay a graduated rule or vernier calipers across the hand just below the fingers and measure the distance. Then measure the length of the finger of Saturn. If these two measurements are exactly the same, the finger is said to be of normal length, or well-developed.

WELL-DEVELOPED FINGER OF SATURN

Key words: balance
　　　　　wisdom
　　　　　loneliness

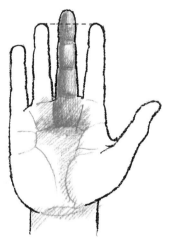

Because of their wisdom and serious nature, true Saturnians can have an enormous influence on society. They approach life in a somber and melancholic manner. Calvin, the preacher from Geneva, is an example of a true Saturnian. In the Netherlands, in particular, the prudery, sternness, and melancholy of Calvinism has dominated the lives of countless people and the influence of this somber Saturnian has been very great. Abraham Lincoln is another example of an influential Saturnian. A senator once said that Lincoln had an air of "great melancholy" about him.

Saturnians are contemplative in their love for other people; they tend to analyze love rather than becoming involved in it. They may be completely taken aback if their partner showers them with feelings. They do not have a reputation as passionate lovers themselves. These people often prefer the solitude of their study to the companionship of others.

Calvin

UNDERDEVELOPED FINGER OF SATURN

Key words: pessimism
           cynicism
           moodiness

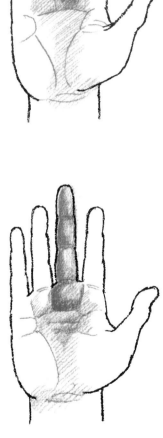

People with a short finger of Saturn (see the illustration) have little inner harmony. Therefore, they often behave in an unbalanced manner and are liable to moodiness.

The serious aspect found in people with a well-developed finger of Saturn degenerates into pessimism in those with an underdeveloped finger of Saturn. Cheerful good humor is foreign to the nature of these people. On the contrary, they make cynical jokes, often at the expense of others. Also, they often take a malicious delight in other people's misfortunes.

The strongest characteristic of Saturnians is their ability to go through life under their own steam. People with an underdeveloped finger of Saturn have lost this ability and are resentful because they are now dependent on others.

OVERDEVELOPED FINGER OF SATURN

Key words: miserliness
           an urge to destroy
           cupidity

People with an overdeveloped mount and finger of Saturn (see the illustration) have a tendency to withdraw into themselves.

All forces of love are excluded from their life and they live with feelings of hate and rancor.

They may lie and threaten and they often direct their hate towards the destruction of people and institutions. They can also be miserly and love to accumulate "filthy lucre."

I have known overdeveloped Saturnians who have caused the downfall of businesses simply through their urge to destroy. In criminological hand analysis, Saturnians with a very over-

developed mount and finger are those who devise complex plans for robbing banks. But the execution of the robbery is generally delegated to people with an overdeveloped Mount of Mars—the Saturnian stays well clear of the action.

The Mount of Apollo (or the Sun) and the Finger of Apollo

APOLLO: God of Prophecy, the Muses, and the Arts

Apollonians have a desire to be of service to their fellow men. This is not so strange because the sun is at the center of our universe and sheds its warmth on everyone.

True Apollonians often radiate like the sun. When the mount and fingers of Apollo are well-developed (see the illustration), then this indicates a natural talent for "brilliant" behavior. In their best form, these people can be mediums and can receive knowledge directly from the "spiritual source."

Apollonians are often enthusiastic, attractive, and inspired people who are also able to inspire others.

Apollo is closely associated with the quality of *love*.

Statue of Apollo, dating from 480 BC

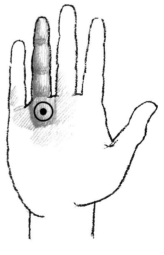

The length of the finger of Apollo is measured by drawing a line across the middle of the first phalanx of the finger of Saturn. If the top of the finger of Apollo reaches above this line, it is regarded as long; if it fails to reach this line, it is regarded as short.

A finger of Apollo a few millimetres longer than normal is regarded as a good sign. The negative aspects only become relevant if the finger is significantly longer. Conversely, in a short finger of Apollo, the few millimetres are of importance.

WELL-DEVELOPED FINGER OF APOLLO

Key words: magnetism
                brilliance
                eloquence

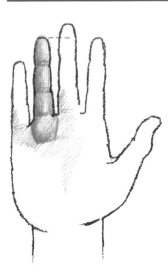

People with a well-developed finger of Apollo (or with one a little longer) are often at the center of attention. This is not strange because, as already stated, the sun is at the center of our planetary system.

Such people attract other people; they have a magnetism and other people gladly bask in their warmth. This can yet again be compared to the sun—we gladly seek the sun so that it can warm us and replenish our energy.

Apollonians are brilliant by nature. They can converse wonderfully on subjects about which they know next to nothing. This is because they possess this knowledge intuitively. They are self-confident and recognize their own talents and also those of others. In addition, Apollonians are happy to be of service to others and like their fellow men to enjoy their radiant energy and to share in the joy of living with them.

These people are usually artistically minded and enjoy beautiful things. Apollo, after all, is the god of the arts and the muses! With their surfeit of energy, they are often good athletes and are born liberal politicians.

Apollonians do not, however, take kindly to restraints.

UNDERDEVELOPED FINGER OF APOLLO

Key words: apathy
            despair
            repellent behavior

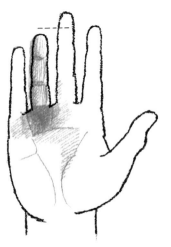

As the radiant light of the sun sinks below the horizon, the world suddenly appears dark and lifeless. And so it is with those who have an underdeveloped finger of Apollo (see the illustration).

These people radiate no light and therefore cannot be at the center of attention. On the contrary, they are among the wallflowers of life—grey and apathetic.

People with such a finger also have a tendency to run away from contact with others.

They have little zest for life; their lack of energy makes

them dispirited and desperate, and they often feel miserable.

These people must learn to take risks in life.

OVERDEVELOPED FINGER OF APOLLO

Key words: recognition
boastfulness
strong opinions

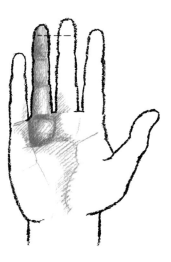

People with an overdeveloped finger of Apollo (see the illustration) have a great desire to shine. They want to be at the center of attention and try to force themselves into this position by telling boastful stories. Their brilliance is corrupted by exaggeration into bragging and conceit.

The energy of the sun is now not used to radiate glory and warmth over other people, but to polish up their own image.

People with an overdeveloped finger of Apollo can put on a dramatic performance in order to obtain the recognition that they need. This ability to be on stage makes them excellent sales and public relations people. In personal relationships, they readily ignore people when they feel that their brilliance or their point of view is not being recognized. But if they themselves are ignored, they often react timidly. As employers they can make great demands on their employees.

They hate to admit that they are wrong because that would damage their brilliant self-image. They expect their fellow men to be just as "perfect" as they are, and this leads to disappointment after disappointment.

Unconsciously they feel that the cosmos contains a wealth of riches and they try to translate that into monetary terms. They are therefore often to be found in capitalistic circles or among wealthy businessmen. Whereas people with a well-developed finger of Apollo take great pleasure in sharing their possessions, people with an overdeveloped finger of Apollo do not. What they have, they prefer to hold onto. They must learn that money does not bring happiness.

The Mount and Finger of Mercury

MERCURY: The Messenger of the Gods and the God of Business and Thieves

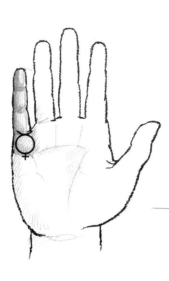

As mentioned earlier, Mercury (see the illustration) ensures that the qualities of the mounts are coordinated and expressed in the world. This mount and its finger therefore indicate the way in which we apply our abilities in practice. We may have many skills, but if Mercury is not in balance, then they cannot be properly applied.

Mercury connotes liberation—a liberation that involves detachment from the physical world. Mercury also inspires our thinking.

True Mercurians are exceptionally inquisitive. They happily "collect" knowledge and bring this knowledge to the other mounts. Therefore, the faculty of memory is also established in Mercury. This faculty of memory, along with knowledge and experience, allows our consciousness to grow.

The finger of Mercury is measured by laying it beside the finger of Apollo. If the tip of the finger of Mercury comes exactly to the crease at the lower end of the first phalanx of the finger of Apollo, then the finger of Mercury is said to be well-developed. If the finger does not reach this line, the millimetres are relevant. A slightly longer finger, however, is just as positive as a slightly longer finger of Apollo.

Mercury is most closely associated with the quality of *wisdom*.

WELL-DEVELOPED FINGER OF MERCURY

Key words: commitment
　　　　　humor
　　　　　communication

Mercurians are active people and are often fast, spontaneous thinkers. They are generally found in the mainstream of life and function extremely well as sharp-witted businesspeople, attorneys, and financiers. It can also be said that they are well suited for occupations that demand a great deal of energy, the ability to communicate, and insight into human nature. Of all the seven planetary types, these people have the best capacity to see through others.

Mercurians must nonetheless resist the temptation to become involved in dubious dealings. It is no coincidence that Mercury (Hermes) was the god of business and of thieves!

A well-developed sense of humor often helps Mercurians to distance themselves from the frustrations of life.

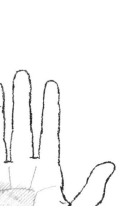

UNDERDEVELOPED FINGER OF MERCURY

Key words: stage fright
poor communication
hesitation

People with a short finger of Mercury (see the illustration) hesitate before they act. They often have good qualities, but they are afraid of putting these qualities into practice. We can compare this feeling with that of an actor who knows his role thoroughly but still suffers from stage fright before his performance.

Nonetheless, these people are still able to perform great deeds once they have summoned up their courage. Then they suddenly hurl themselves into the task at hand and soon have it finished.

The stage fright of the Mercurian can also find expression in overcompensation. This can occur especially if they also have an overdeveloped Mars negative or positive. They shout out loud because they are actually afraid to open their mouth. Due to this tendency to overcompensate, people with a short finger of Mercury often come

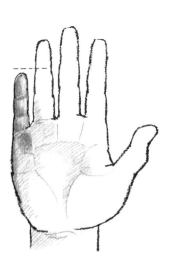

across to others in the wrong way. Many people think that they are insolent, while exactly the reverse is true.

Because they are afraid to show what they are capable of, they invent all kinds of wonderful excuses. In particular, they invent phony illnesses because illness is readily accepted as an excuse in our world.

In the Hasta Samudrika Shastra, *the Mount of Mercury is named* Buddhi, *which means an enlightened state of mind and detachment from all desires and intellectual illusions. In spiritual centers I often hear people saying that we must be detached. But in my opinion, we must find a balance between attachment and detachment. There is a behavior pattern called "neurotic detachment" and I do not regard this as a virtue. In negative detachment, we have feelings of isolation and reserve; Jung termed such a situation* ichverhaftung *(ego imprisonment).*

In my practice I often receive clients who tell me that they want to be free and so do not enter into relationships. But in reality they are afraid of committing themselves. I try to explain to these people that freedom means liberation from fear so that they have the freedom to commit themselves to others or to become involved in the activities of life. These people often hesitate because they are unconsciously afraid of making mistakes if they become too involved with people or activities.

Thus, the conventional wisdom "We learn from our mistakes" needs to be realized by people who have a short finger of Mercury.

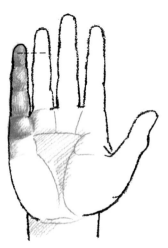

OVERDEVELOPED FINGER OF MERCURY

Key words: cunning
          restlessness
          unscrupulousness

In the holy book of the Hindus, the *Bhagavad Gita,* the Lord Krishna gave the following instructions to his disciple Arjuna: "Therefore, without being attached to the fruits of activities, one should act as a matter of duty, for by working without attachment one attains the supreme." This verse contains wisdom that people with an overdeveloped finger of Mercury should take to heart. These people are far too attached to the material results of their efforts. They can be calculating and cunning, and want to earn as much money as possible as quickly as possible.

They talk in an animated way and have a tendency to be continually on the go.

These people find it easy to be unfaithful in relationships.

Through my knowledge of criminological hand analysis, I know that people with a very overdeveloped finger of Mercury are sometimes involved in share swindles or in the setting up of "paper" companies. In this way, they use their "golden tongue" and their insight into people and situations to enrich themselves in a cunning and crafty manner. In fact, they are often so cunning that the police have difficulty in finding sufficient proof to prosecute them.

★　　★　　★

An old piece of conventional wisdom in the form of a rhyme I still remember from my childhood offers a striking example of the significance of the thumb and the fingers.

"To bed, to bed, said Tommy Thumb (the thumb).
First let's eat, said the Greedy One (Jupiter).
Where can we find food? said Long John (Saturn).
In Grandma's cupboard, said Ring-a-ling (Apollo).
I'll tell on you! said Little Thing (Mercury)."

As already stated, the thumb reflects the human will and urges people to act. The Jupiterian enjoys good food. The Saturnian is the seeker, who asks questions about life. The Apollonian knows the answer to every question and the Mercurian is balanced between honesty and dishonesty.

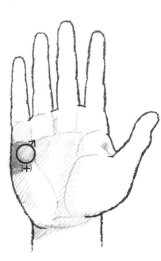

The Mount of Mars Positive

MARS: God of War

Earlier in this chapter, I stated that Mars negative provided for bodily resistance and power and Mars positive (see the illustration) for mental resilience. We need both types of power in this life.

Mars positive is most closely associated with the quality of *will*.

Since Mars positive has no finger, we will examine the mount itself.

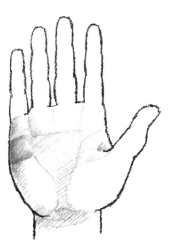

WELL-DEVELOPED MOUNT OF MARS POSITIVE

Key words: perseverance
               stability
               self-control

The mental strength of Mars positive supports the attributes of the other mounts and fingers (see the illustration). People with a well-developed Mars positive are also often a source of power and stability to those around them. They are very protective as well. Mars positive gives people an enthusiastic, purposeful, and calm approach to life, coupled with a healthy perseverance.

UNDERDEVELOPED MOUNT OF MARS POSITIVE

Key words: fear of disappointment
               apathy
               self-destructiveness

People with an underdeveloped Mars positive (see the illustration) do not have the mental resilience of those with a well-developed Mars positive. They unconsciously expect disappointments from life and this gives them an apathetic attitude and feelings of despair. They see no viable future. When people expect disappointments, they either attract them or create them themselves by sending out negative thoughts.

They can also feel hounded by people who mean them well and who want to incite them to action. This hounded feeling can be expressed in uncontrolled outbursts of anger, which can sometimes manifest itself in physical violence.

At worst, their feelings of despair can lead to self-destructive behavior. They behave in such a manner that all the positive elements in their life disappear.

I sometimes see children in my practice who refuse to learn at school because they see the future in a completely negative way. I have also seen people who have been fired because they were inactive and showed a lack of enthusiasm for their work.

These people should take the saying "Where there's life, there's hope" to heart. During a consultation or in therapy, I help them to develop positive expectations from life. Hope brings forth positive expectations and a feeling of optimism. Just think of the surge of energy we experience when we anticipate an upcoming vacation.

OVERDEVELOPED MOUNT OF MARS POSITIVE

Key words: explosive temperament
              unreasonableness
              possessiveness

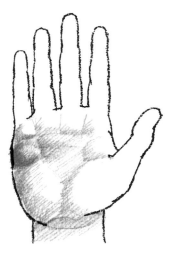

In the first place it must be stated that an overdeveloped Mars positive is very uncommon (see the illustration). But when it does occur, it indicates very domineering mental power, which can degenerate into mental aggression. People with this trait are often sarcastic and blindly press ahead with whatever is in their mind at the time. They regard their partners as possessions and differences in opinion or suspected unfaithfulness are not always solved by means of rational discussion.

As I mentioned earlier, in evolutionary hand analysis I work with combinations. The art is to decipher the true links between the positive and negative qualities of the mounts in the hand.

With mounts I look particularly at the most dominating one together with the finger that belongs to it. The traits revealed by this dominating mount are indicative of a large part of our behavior.

I then decipher the links between this positive or negative dominating mount with the positive and negative qualities of the other mounts in order of importance, and also with the other signs in the hand.

The mounts often represent unconscious qualities. The art is to make the unconscious conscious so that people can work on it and with it.

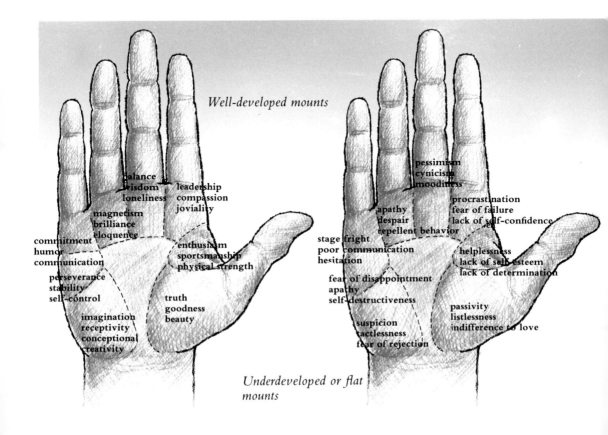

Well-developed mounts

balance
wisdom
loneliness · leadership
compassion
joviality
magnetism
brilliance
eloquence
commitment
humor
communication
enthusiasm
sportsmanship
physical strength
perseverance
stability
self-control
imagination
receptivity
conceptional
creativity
truth
goodness
beauty

pessimism
cynicism
moodiness
procrastination
fear of failure
lack of self-confidence
apathy
despair
repellent behavior
stage fright
poor communication
hesitation
helplessness
lack of self-esteem
lack of determination
fear of disappointment
apathy
self-destructiveness
passivity
listlessness
indifference to love
suspicion
tactlessness
fear of rejection

Underdeveloped or flat mounts

Mars, god of war

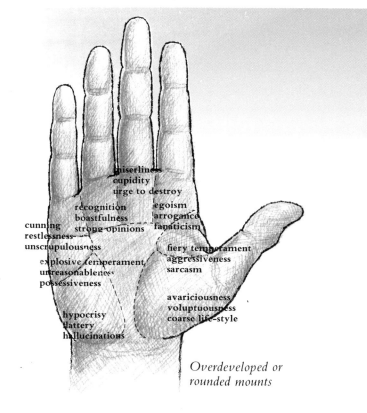

miserliness
cupidity
urge to destroy

recognition   egoism
boastfulness   arrogance
cunning   strong opinions   fanaticism
restlessness
unscrupulousness

         fiery temperament
         aggressiveness
explosive temperament   sarcasm
unreasonableness
possessiveness

         avariciousness
         voluptuousness
hypocrisy   coarse life-style
flattery
hallucinations

*Overdeveloped or
rounded mounts*

7·PRIMARY LINES

In "The Creation of Adam," a ceiling fresco by Michelangelo, the finger of God imparts the divine spark to the Jupiter finger of Adam, thus giving life to the lifeless hand.

A similar sort of process takes place in billions of nerve cells in the human brain. Every brain cell produces electrochemical energy that, in a manner of speaking, jumps like a spark through the "nerve finger" of the nerve cell to the "nerve finger" of the next nerve cell. This process continues endlessly. In this way, electrical currents are formed, which travel along the pathways of the nervous system.

These electrical impulses (energy) give us consciousness and enable us to think, feel, move, and observe the world around us.

By way of the nerve ends, the electrical current from our "thought energy" cuts lines in our hands.

The fingers and mounts are likewise connected neurologically with specific areas of the brain. The development and function-

"The Creation of Adam"

ing of these areas determine the development or lack of development of the mounts and fingers.

The philosopher Immanuel Kant stated that "hands are externalized brains." Each part of the brain has a particular function. The way in which the different parts function together determines our character and behavior, which can be seen in our hands.

Metaphorically we can compare the working of the brain to the functioning of an organization with many departments, which are all linked to each other by telephone lines. Because these departments work together, the organization is able to create products or services.

In a similar way, electrical channels link the different areas of the brain. Data and instructions that determine behavior (the product) pass along these "telephone lines." Lines also run from mount to mount in the palm of the hand. These lines inform us how the different areas of the brain are linked to each other and how they work together on spiritual, intellectual, emotional, and physical levels.

Returning to the analogy of an organization, when, for example, the marketing department grows and moves to another location, a new telephone line must be laid. I think that a similar process takes place in the brain. As people grow and develop, new electrochemical links are formed and thus the lines in the hand change. Some disappear and new ones are created.

A plastic surgeon recently told me that during operations he sometimes had to replace the skin on his patients' palms. It struck him that the lines that were there before later reappeared. This indicates that the lines are not located coincidentally at certain places in the hand. Likewise, neither is the development of the mounts accidental, and can be seen to change as the person changes.

With few exceptions, the palm of the hand contains three basic lines—the line of the Heart, the line of the Head, and the line of Life (see the illustration on page 106).

These lines are linked with the three basic qualities of love, wisdom, and will, which were described in the chapter concerning the thumb. The quality of love is

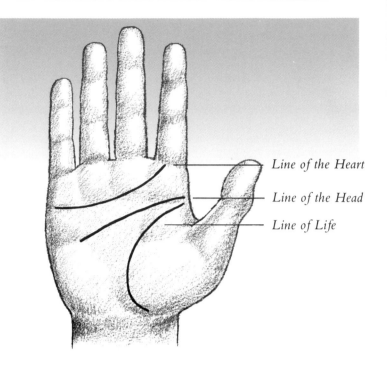

Line of the Heart

Line of the Head

Line of Life

found in the line of the Heart; this line indicates our emotional strength. Wisdom (the ability to reason) has found a home in the line of the Head. This line gives indications of our intellectual strength and of the way in which we control our life. Will is seated in the line of Life and manifests itself as our life force, instincts, and physical strength.

These three lines have a deeper connection with our subconscious than the other lines in the palm and therefore change less quickly.

The easiest way to explain the significance of these three lines is to discuss them in terms of evolution and the working of the brain. The structure of the brain is extremely complicated. In order to arrive at a clear explanation, it's best to roughly divide it into three sections that lie in layers, one over the other. These three layers (shown in the illustration) indicate the three phases of development in the evolution of the brain.

The first layer, called the reptilian brain, or "old brain," we have in common with creatures such as snakes, lizards, and tortoises. This part of the brain con-

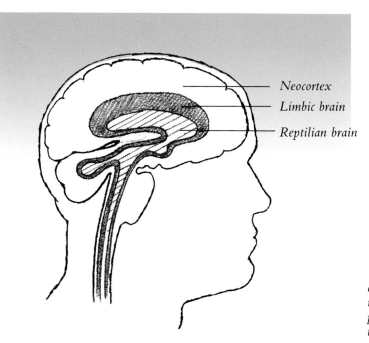

Neocortex
Limbic brain
Reptilian brain

These parts of the brain at different levels are linked by rising and falling neural pathways—the projection tracks.

sists of the matrix of the brain stem, the midbrain, the basal ganglia, and much of the hypothalamus. Encircling this part of the brain is the limbic brain, or the "emotional brain." This we have in common with lower mammals such as rats, rabbits, and horses. The neocortex, or "thinking cap," is positioned around the limbic brain. This part of the brain is highly developed in primates such as chimpanzees and most especially Homo sapiens (thinking man).

The reptilian brain functions as a sort of biocomputer and regulates our reflexes. It reacts immediately to incoming stimuli and houses our instincts so that we can survive physically, feel physical well-being, and develop our muscular strength. In short, this part of the brain controls all physical aspects.

This brain was the first brain to regulate the life force, or life energy, known to the Hindus as *jeevan*. In the *Hasta Samudrika Shastra,* the term for the line of Life is *jeevan rekha* (*rekha* means line).

This line shows how we use our life force in this life. Indications of events that interfere with the life stream—

illness, for example—can also be found in this line. In addition, it shows whether we approach life willingly or with reluctance. Although the line of Life primarily reflects the physical aspects of our life, it also yields information on aspects of our psychological and spiritual makeup.

The limbic brain registers pain and aversion, among other things, and stimulates such patterns of behavior as care, aggression, affection, happiness, and sadness. It also reacts to reward and punishment. All of this is reflected in the line of the Heart.

This line supplies information concerning both our feelings and emotions as well as the physical health of our heart. Spiritual and psychological aspects, such as the evolution of one's soul and instinctive occurrences, can also be read from this line.

The brain that was developed last, the neocortex, or "thinking cap," gives us the ability to say "I," and thus the means to consciously relate to the outside world. This ability is what differentiates us from animals.

In the *Hasta Samudrika Shastra,* the line of the Head is named the *mustishk rekha. Mustishk* means the brain that gives us our individuality and controls the nervous and sensory systems. (*Rekha* again means line.) The neocortex is that part of the brain in which conscious control and coordination of the other parts of the brain take place. The workings of the brain can be compared to the hierarchy in an army. The general (neocortex) directs, controls, and coordinates the officers and men (the other parts of the brain).

Drunkenness demonstrates the importance of this part of the brain. Large quantities of alcohol lessen its conscious and controlling functions. Our moral feelings coarsen, we lose control over our movements, and our capacity for judgment and self-criticism is adversely affected.

The neocortex, represented by the line of the Head, gives us the gift of directing (and potentially purifying) our wishes and actions through free will and the power of thought. The German philosopher Hegel wrote: "It is thought that transforms the soul into the spirit." By this he meant that our capacity to think can lead us to our spiritual potential or our inner source. The Yogis are striking examples of this, as they are able to control their bodily functions with their spiritual energy.

According to Buddhist teachings, in a perfect Buddha the three primary lines form a circle in the palm of the hand, called the *dharma chakra*. The circle represents the alpha and omega, the source and the return to the macrocosm through the cycles of involution and evolution.

As has already been stated, the reptilian brain is the source of the line of Life and so this line primarily reflects the physical powers of man.

Under the guidance of the neocortex's refined intelligence, however, the line of Life also shows that we do not live to eat, but that we eat in order to live. This line shows us motivation, the joy of life, and the quality of life. When the line of Life is saturated, as it were, with higher values, it then reflects our growth from a point where we were only concerned with ourselves to a point where we use our life force for the benefit of others.

This principle also applies to the line of the Heart. When influenced by the "I consciousness," represented by the line of the Head, emotions become purified. The line of the Heart, among other things, indicates how far our soul has advanced along the evolutionary path from pure lust to altruistic love.

Besides information about the manner in which we control our life and about our intelligence, the line of the Head also yields information concerning our ability to concentrate, the flexibility (or inflexibility) of our approach to life, and so on. There will be more about this later in the chapter.

It is of great importance to the balanced functioning of a person that neither of the three parts of the brain dominate, but that each is in balance with the others.

The shape of the hand can also be linked with the three parts of the brain (see the illustration on page 110).

The base of the palm is most closely associated with the reptilian brain—the physical aspects of man. In the illus-

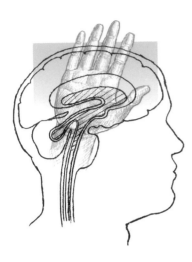

tration, this part of the brain is depicted in the base of the hand. People with a spatulate hand, which is broader at the base, therefore tend to concentrate on the physical aspects of life.

Sociability and a dynamic approach to life, in addition to many other attributes, are determined by the limbic brain. This brain is reflected in the upper part of the palm. People with a square hand, or a broad palm, demonstrate these qualities, along with the quality of practical thinking.

In the illustration, the fingers are depicted in the neocortex, the part of the brain that makes it possible for us to think at a high level. People with a philosophical hand (with longer, knottier fingers) are stimulated through this part of the brain.

We must, however, be aware that every hand shape is related to some degree to every part of the brain. The elementary hand, for example, has the strongest connection with the reptilian brain, then with the limbic brain, and lastly with the neocortex.

This diagram shows how corresponding areas in the hemispheres are linked by nerve tracks. These nerve tracks pass through the corpus callosum, the bridge that binds the two cerebral hemispheres together.

Association fibres (nerve tracks) that link areas of the same cerebral hemisphere.

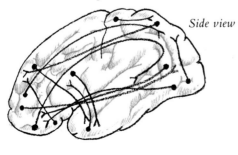

Side view

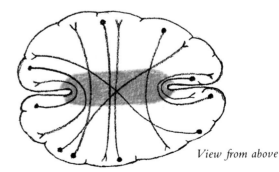

View from above

The lines are the energy links between the different mounts and they symbolize the interaction of the different parts of the brain.

It is of great importance to observe exactly where a line begins (arises) and where it ends. The beginning of a line indicates the institution or the intention, the further course of the line shows the direction of the energy, and the end of the line signifies the eventual purpose. The following analogy may help to clarify this concept. Somebody wants to achieve something (intention) for a political party (institution). He formulates a plan (direction) to achieve the result (purpose) he wants.

The three primary lines begin at the thumb side of the hand. The thumb represents our divine source. The word "character" has Greek origins and is related to the verbs meaning "to grind," "to scratch," and "to engrave." The primary lines are engraved, as it were, through the unconscious and therefore do not change as quickly as secondary lines (which are discussed in greater detail in the following chapter). The qualities and habits that the secondary lines represent are etched less deeply into the character. These lines are related to preconsciousness and consciousness and thus change more quickly; they can also appear as new lines or disappear completely. The term "preconsciousness" refers to the knowledge or qualities that are readily available to our consciousness. If we are reading a book, for example, at that moment we do not need to know how to drive. But as soon as we climb into a car, that knowledge flows back into our consciousness.

A palm in which many lines crisscross (see the print) has, in proportion, too many secondary lines (preconscious and conscious lines). People with such a hand therefore live too much in their waking consciousness. They think that as long as they are watchful and keep their head, everything will be fine. But this is not the case. The deeper layers of wisdom and knowledge are housed in the unconscious and these people do not allow them to flow to the surface. The result is that they are often restless and lack direction. One might say that they run around like a chicken with its head cut off. These people should learn to trust their inner wisdom and take time to consider before they act.

This phenomenon is one of the paradoxes of the human psyche. People are afraid of losing control over their own life. This fear affects their thinking, which in turn causes them to lose control over their life!

Broad, shallow lines

Narrow, deep lines

Narrow, shallow lines

The Quality of the Lines

It is important to observe whether the lines are deep, wide, or narrow. The significance of the quality of the lines can perhaps be better understood if we compare the stream of energy that the lines conduct with the flow of water in a river. This water flows more slowly and less powerfully where the river is wide than it does where it is narrow.

Broad, shallow lines indicate a slow stream of energy. People with these lines are physically disposed and are generally interested in sports and the outdoor life.

Narrow, deep lines connote an intense, concentrated stream of energy. People with these lines have deep, keen interests; they are interested in the higher things in life.

Narrow, shallow lines represent a weak, superficial stream of energy. People with these lines have no deeply felt convictions and do not possess very much physical or mental energy.

Lines that are broken indicate an irregular and disturbed stream of energy. The nature of the disturbance depends on the meaning of the line.

An island in a line indicates blocked energy. The nature of the block is also dependent on the meaning of the line.

Interrupted lines

Island in a line

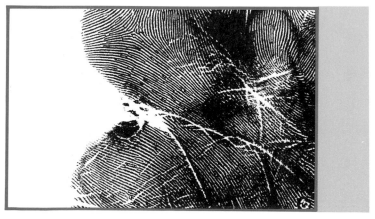

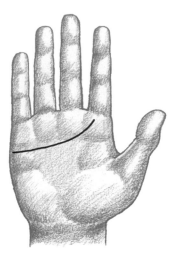

The Line of the Heart

Key words: emotional and sexual power
        attitude to love (idealistic, realistic, egoistic, sensual)
        indication of the condition of the heart

The line of the Heart (see the illustration) provides information about a person's emotional strengths and feelings. All these feelings stem from the quality of *love*. Indeed, love is the root of all emotions. From emotion a person must "grow back," as it were, to the root of pure love.

The whole spectrum of feelings, from a lack of self-love to unselfish, altruistic love, is expressed in the Heart line. For this reason, we can also read the state of the evolution of the soul from this line, in conjunction with other markings. The line of the Heart can begin (arise) in the Mount of Jupiter, in the Mount of Saturn, or in Mars negative.

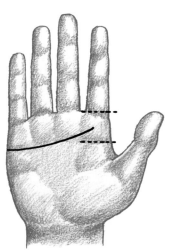

LINE OF THE HEART ARISES IN THE CENTER OF JUPITER

When the line of the Heart arises exactly in the center of the Mount of Jupiter (see the illustration), then it is "ideally" developed. In the process of evolution, the line of the Heart grows slowly towards this ideal. If the Heart line begins in the center of Jupiter, it indicates exceptional spirituality. It also indicates that we can understand the macrocosm and take it into our heart. Emotions, feelings, and love are then purified.

People with such a line of Heart are capable of altruistic love and put their spiritual qualities to the service of others. They have a very pure emotional life and are able to receive very clear intuitions.

In short, the line of the Heart arising in the center of Jupiter is a sign of an advanced state of being. The well-known Indian sage Krishnamurti had such a line.

LINE OF THE HEART ARISES IN UPPER JUPITER

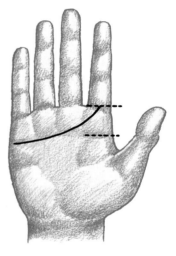

The upper part of the Mount of Jupiter represents mental energy. If the line of the Heart arises here (see the illustration), this mental energy influences one's emotional life. Since Jupiter is also an idealistic mount, the emotional life of people with such a Heart line thus has an idealistic, intellectual streak.

Such people could be idealistic revolutionaries or starry-eyed do-gooders. They may read idealistic literature, for example, and expect their partners to do the same.

If we are overidealistic and foster such great expectations, however, we are often faced with disappointments.

LINE OF THE HEART ARISES IN LOWER JUPITER

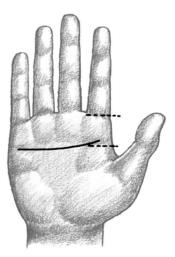

This part of the Mount of Jupiter (see the illustration) reflects the physical world. The ideals of a person with the line of the Heart arising here are not so lofty but much more down to earth.

For this reason, such people usually enjoy earthly pleasures, including sex. If they do not obtain these pleasures, they frequently manipulate others in order to impose their will.

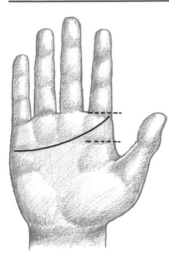

LINE OF THE HEART ARISES IN UPPER JUPITER TOWARDS THE THUMB

In this case, the influence of the thumb affects the intensity of the emotions. In people with such a line of the Heart (see the illustration), this intensity is both emotionally and intellectually directed. They have an emotionally charged, intellectual approach to life and are often inundated with idealistic feelings. They may engage others, for example, in intense conversation in an attempt to convince them of the validity of their ideas.

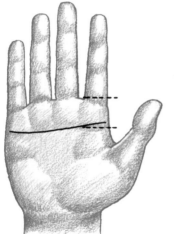

LINE OF THE HEART ARISES IN LOWER JUPITER TOWARDS THE THUMB

The intensive emotions are now more physically directed. When the line falls quite steeply (see the illustration), these intense emotions are concerned with sexuality. These people therefore experience their sexuality intensely, which often results in possessiveness.

In general, overintense emotions are not good. They create tension in oneself and arouse opposition in others.

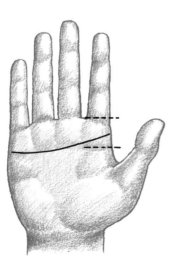

LINE OF THE HEART ARISES IN THE CENTER OF JUPITER TOWARDS THE THUMB

The emotions of these people are still intense. This intensity is not specifically emotionally or intellectually directed, however; but instead lies between the two (see the illustration).

LINE OF THE HEART ARISES IN MIDDLE JUPITER TOWARDS MERCURY

The intensity diminishes. People with a Heart line like this (see the illustration) do not experience such intense emotions. Instead they are more reserved and earnest and are inclined to take their relationships very seriously.

LINE OF THE HEART ARISES IN LOWER JUPITER TOWARDS MERCURY

These people (see the illustration) are more directed to the material aspects of life. Their daily life is of the highest importance to them. The material side and the other practical advantages of a relationship are more important to them than the idealistic aspects.

LINE OF THE HEART ARISES IN MARS NEGATIVE

When the line of the Heart arises in Mars negative (see the illustration), there is almost invariably a question of suppressed anger. These people have experienced something in the past (in a previous life) to which they still react in an emotional and angry manner.

People with such a Heart line also have a deeply rooted need for attention. The way in which they demand attention can be seen from other aspects of the hand.

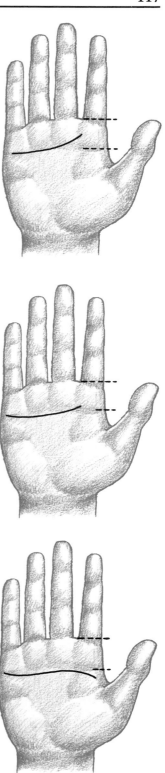

Overdeveloped Jupiter:	behave haughtily
Short Jupiter:	arouse irritation
Overdeveloped Apollo:	cold-shoulder others
Underdeveloped Apollo:	waste away or pine
Overdeveloped Saturn:	shake it off and immerse themselves still deeper in their thoughts
Overdeveloped Luna:	behave pathetically
Overdeveloped Mercury:	begin to nag and cling
Overdeveloped Mars:	threaten
Underdeveloped Mars:	feign helplessness

Naturally, these are not the best of ways of soliciting attention. It's best to simply say that we need it.

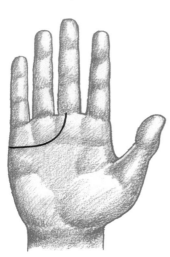

LINE OF THE HEART ARISES IN UPPER SATURN

Life presses heavily on the spirit of people with such a line of the Heart. We can tell that they take life very seriously because the line of the Heart (see the illustration) arises in the intellectual part of this mount. They also take relationships too seriously and do not seem to realize that now and again they need to "lighten up."

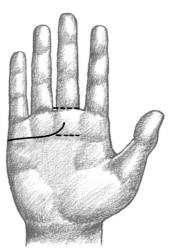

LINE OF THE HEART ARISES IN THE CENTER OF SATURN

If the line of the Heart arises in the center of the Mount of Saturn, it indicates that the person is very self-centered, unfeeling, and cold. It also indicates that the status of a well-off partner could be sufficient reason for him or her to pursue a marriage.

If a thin line linking this line with Jupiter can be seen, however, this is an indication that consciousness is growing. But if the line is not deep enough, it means that these people can fall back into old patterns of behavior.

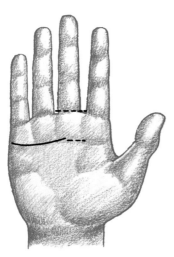

LINE OF THE HEART ARISES IN LOWER SATURN

People with such a Heart line (see the illustration) have a tendency to become involved in a number of relationships with sexual undertones. They try to discover the meaning of love by taking one partner after another. If this tendency cannot be expressed in deed, it is expressed in thought.

LINE OF THE HEART ARISES IN SATURN TOWARDS MERCURY

This Heart line (see the illustration) signifies that there is little strength in the heart. The life energy is found in the head and not the heart. Because they don't have much energy in their heart, people with such a line have little love to give. They have cut themselves off from their inner source. They feel abandoned and therefore yearn for love, but their head tends to speak in place of their heart.

LINE OF THE HEART ARISES BETWEEN UPPER JUPITER AND UPPER SATURN

This Heart line begins between Jupiter and Saturn (see the illustration). These people therefore possess both the idealism of Jupiter and the seriousness of Saturn. Thus, they are idealistic and serious in their relationships with others. Because of this, they entertain extremely high expectations—sometimes so high that no one can fulfill them. They almost inevitably create an area of tension between the ideal and the reality.

People with such a Heart line strive for perfection within themselves and look for it within their fellow men.

Women who have such a line, for example, can be overanxious mothers. In their desire to do everything right, they tend to bring up their children with too much involvement.

LINE OF THE HEART ARISES BETWEEN THE CENTER OF JUPITER AND THE CENTER OF SATURN

People with this Heart line (see the illustration) regard their relationships in a realistic manner—between the idealistic and the practical.

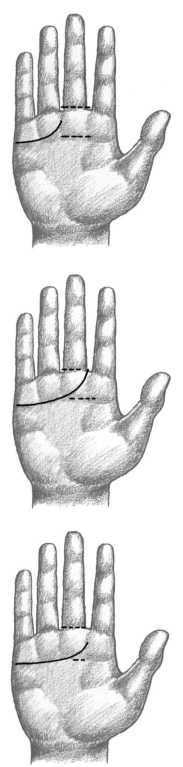

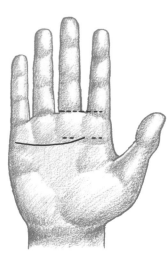

LINE OF THE HEART ARISES BETWEEN LOWER JUPITER AND LOWER SATURN

The relationships of people with such a line (see the illustration) usually have sexual undertones. These people must learn that one of the purposes of a relationship is to achieve harmony between the sexual and the spiritual.

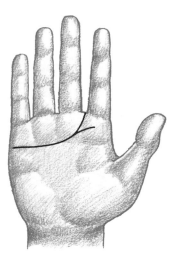

LINE OF THE HEART IS FORKED WHERE IT ARISES

If the Heart line arises in a fork (see the illustration), it means that the powers of the places in the mounts where these lines begin are united with each other.

For example, if one line begins between upper Jupiter and upper Saturn and the other begins between the center of Jupiter and the center of Saturn, then the high idealism of the upper line is tempered by the more realistic streak of the lower line.

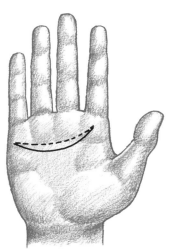

BOWED LINE OF THE HEART

If the Heart line curves quite deeply downwards (see the illustration), it indicates a warm nature. If the line bows too deeply, then it is no longer in its own "territory," as it were. It seeks support from the qualities of another line—in this case, the line of the Head. These people tend to rationalize because their feelings are dominated by their mental powers. They place too much trust in their logic and not enough in their warm spontaneity. If the line of the Heart curves very deeply downwards, the emotional behavior becomes still more calculating. One's intellect assumes the upper hand and directs the expression of one's feelings.

STRAIGHT LINE OF THE HEART

People with such a Heart line (see the illustration) express their feelings in a cool way. Their behavior is cool because the Heart line is pulled towards the fingers and the fingers represent mental powers.

EXTRA LINE OF THE HEART

This extra Heart line (see the illustration) is known as a "sister line" and it strengthens the qualities of the Heart line. People with this extra line possess greater emotional strength. This, in turn, means that they have greater stability because they can control their emotions better. An extra Heart line can also indicate that these people long to attract partners who can offer them emotional support in a relationship.

THE SIMIAN LINE

Here, the line of the Heart and the line of the Head have fused together. This indicates that the ability to reason and the ability to feel are not divorced from each other. However, it is best if these two areas—thinking and feeling—function separately, otherwise harmony is disturbed and confusion is created.

The probable cause of this fusion is a panic reaction to some emotional shock. This panic was locked tightly into the person's subconscious and never released. Although the crisis occurred in a previous life, in this life the person's thoughts are still unconsciously directed towards it. At moments of tension, he or she can panic again.

The mental images from the past that are locked into the mind deluge, as it were, the heart. It sometimes happens that such people can rid themselves of the tension by becoming hysterical or by physically destroying something.

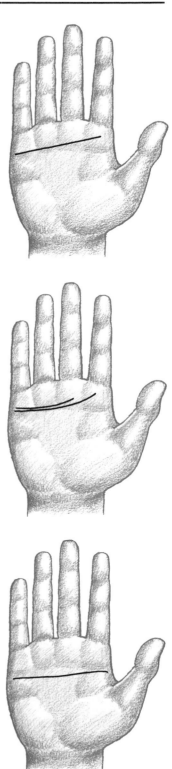

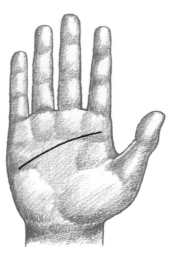

The Line of the Head

Key words: intellectual power
responsibility for ourself

The line of the Head (see the illustration) reflects the direction in our life. Because we possess consciousness, we direct our life with our mind. We are blessed with a conscious state of mind and this means that we are responsible for our actions. This sense of responsibility stems from our having been given intelligence. In contrast, animals have no conscious state of mind; they act instinctively.

The line of the Head has direct contact with the neocortex. This part of the brain gives us an ego, or a sense of our individuality.

The line of the Head indicates our dualistic, analytical mode of thinking. Thinking is the coordination and processing of the stream of information obtained from our senses—from seeing, hearing, smelling, touching, and tasting. We hear, for example, a particular sound and in our mind's eye we immediately see an image of a trumpet. Our mind therefore contains the concept of a trumpet. The more we develop intellectually, the greater the number of concepts we have in our mind. We continually weigh these concepts against what we perceive and in this way we learn. The fact that we weigh concepts against perceptions is the reason this mode of thinking is known as dualistic.

Thinking also determines behavior; we act after we have thought. If we do not act, we do not undergo experiences and then we learn nothing in this life. If we do act, however, we are motivated by a cause and then it goes without saying that we are faced with an effect. The inner causes (the beginning of the line) and the mode of thinking by which we want to be effective (the end of the line) can be found in the line of the Head. As previously stated, this line represents our dualistic, analytical mode of thinking. This is in contrast to monistic thinking, which is of a higher order.

Monistic thinking flows directly in us, as it were. It is an understanding without form, a direct knowing, in which our actions are influenced by inspiration. This inspiration, however, takes form as soon as we allow this energy to flow to the brain and manifest as thinking.

LINE OF THE HEAD MERGES WITH LINE OF LIFE

Ideally, the lines in the hand should stand apart. When lines touch, the different energies merge and that is not their intention.

Since the line of the Head represents our mental energy and the line of Life represents our physical energy, if the two lines merge (see the illustration), it indicates that thinking is influenced by a physical consciousness. People with these merging lines worry too much about how they are seen physically by other people. They are too focused on their physical expression in this world. They are easily embarrassed and therefore behave in a timid, self-conscious manner. They are also afraid of being hurt.

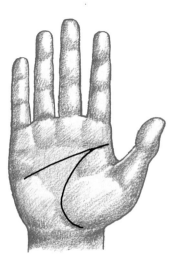

But all facets in this life have both positive and negative aspects. The positive aspect for these people is that they are sensitive to the feelings of others and do not hold other people up to ridicule. They themselves know all too well how that feels. The disadvantage, however, is that they tend to worry too much about other people.

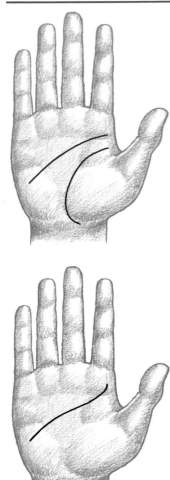

LINE OF THE HEAD IS SOME DISTANCE FROM LINE OF LIFE

The further the Head line is from the Life line (see the illustration), the more independent the thinking process. People with some distance between these two lines are independent thinkers and remain aloof from the sensitivities of others. Therefore, they sometimes exert a calming influence amid the "dramas" of life.

They do not concern themselves with what other people say about them, because they are generally quite unaware of how they appear to others. These people have little consideration for others and so their remarks and opinions are generally delivered straight from the shoulder. However, in the long run, other people will not put up with their behavior. Those with such lines often learn consideration for others the hard way.

LINE OF THE HEAD ARISES IN JUPITER

The entire thinking process of people with such a line (see the illustration) is colored by the idealism of Jupiter. Their overall pattern of thinking is ambitious and they invest a great deal of mental energy in achieving particular ideals or personal ambitions.

If they are overambitious, however, this often proves to be a negative quality. Ideals that are too high can rarely be realized.

LINE OF THE HEAD ARISES IN SATURN

Saturn ensures that thinking is filled with somberness and melancholy. People with such a line (see the illustration) therefore think in an exceptionally serious manner. They find little joy in life and usually turn everything into a problem. In short, they are continually finding fault.

LINE OF THE HEAD ARISES IN MARS NEGATIVE

Such a line (see the illustration) indicates suppressed anger.

If Mars negative is underdeveloped, it connotes a lack of decisiveness, and this is also expressed in the mental processes. People with such a line arising from an under-developed mount tend to think little of themselves and feel powerless.

Whether Mars negative is underdeveloped or overde-veloped, people with this line sometimes manifest defen-sive or aggressive behavior.

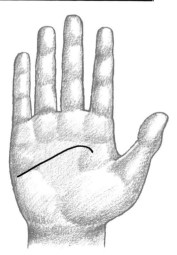

A SMALL LENGTH MISSING WHERE THE LINE OF THE HEAD ARISES

People with this missing length (see the illustration) were probably very docile children, because such a line indi-cates that they only began to develop their own initiative at a later stage in life.

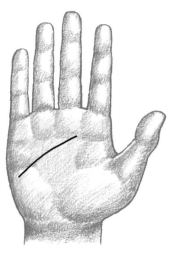

LINE OF THE HEAD ENDS IN MARS POSITIVE

Such a line (see the illustra-tion) indicates that that person thinks in a down-to-earth and analytical manner.

If the Head line is long and curls upwards at the end, the curl is then located in Mercury (see the illustration). Mercury represents, among other things, coordination, and so the thinking of people with such a line is directed towards coordination. They want to see clear links between various phenomena and often have a talent for organization.

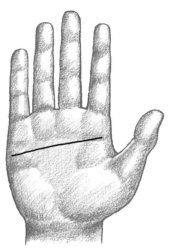

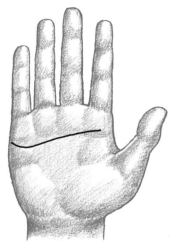

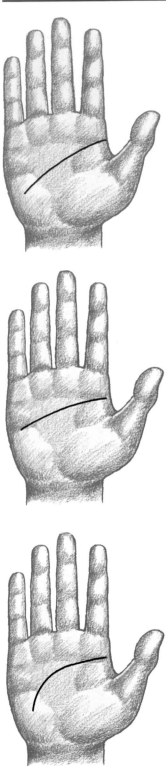

LINE OF THE HEAD ENDS IN THE CENTER OF LUNA

Receptivity to ideas is reflected in Luna. People with a Head line ending in the center of Luna (see the illustration) are therefore creative thinkers. They are able to pick up an idea very quickly and can immediately do something with it.

They also react quickly to things that they observe with their senses because they do not take long to assimilate them. They are therefore less circumspect than analytical thinkers, who consider things for a longer period of time in order to analyze them more fully.

In addition, they are often in tune with the thoughts of other people. People with such a line are sensitive thinkers and often make outstanding therapists.

LINE OF THE HEAD ENDS BETWEEN MARS POSITIVE AND LUNA

This is a marvellous line, because people with such a line are both creative and analytical. They sense, for example, what other people want, are able to analyze it, and then react appropriately to it.

LINE OF THE HEAD ENDS IN LOWER LUNA

The mental power now gravitates towards self-pity. The life of people with such a line of the Head (see the illustration) is subconsciously directed towards creating situations for themselves that become a shambles. They are continually faced with problems and their thinking unconsciously attracts unpleasant situations.

The power of self-pity is the opposite pole from the power of love. These people wallow in self-pity. They wish to change this, but at the same time they do not. They may consult a therapist or a healer but do not persevere with treatment so that they give no one a chance to actually help them.

The extreme of self-pity is self-destruction and, in fact, that is what these people are engaged in. Sometimes this reaches such an extreme that they even consider suicide.

It is very difficult to break these people out of their vicious circle. What we can do is try to persuade them to think logically. When this line ends in an overdeveloped lower Luna, these self-destructive feelings can be particularly strong. Moreover, if the line originates in Saturn, there are also often feelings of melancholy.

This is an example of a line linked to the reptilian brain. As has already been explained, this part of the brain is concerned with instinctive behavior and survival and does not have the capacity for logical thought. Because they do not first think logically, people with this line find themselves in positions in which they are on the defensive. The direction and the end of the line draw them, as it were, towards this primitive part of the brain.

LINE OF THE HEAD ENDS ABOVE MARS POSITIVE TOWARDS MERCURY

People with such a line (see the illustration) experience a restriction of consciousness because the distance between the line of the Head and the line of the Heart is small. Feeling and thinking are not in balance because there is no spaciousness or openness. These people view their life in an overemotional manner, as indicated by the line of the Head being drawn towards the line of the Heart. In addition, they tend to see things in a narrow-minded manner.

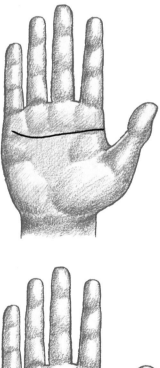

SHORT LINE OF THE HEAD

People with a short line of the Head (see the illustration) generally have the necessary qualities to accumulate material possessions in a practical manner. They have few intellectual interests.

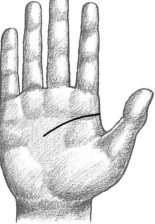

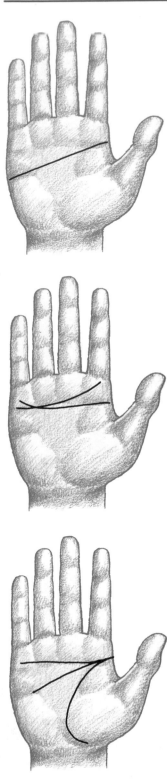

LONG LINE OF THE HEAD

The longer the line of the Head (see the illustration), the more abstract the thinking. People with a long Head line bring more depth into their thinking because they can retain their thoughts for longer periods. For this reason, their thinking is largely intellectually directed.

People with a long, straight line of the Head often retreat into their own thoughts, from which they look out contemplatively on the world around them. They think, however, in hypotheses and neglect the input of their intuition. Thinking is naturally important, but the highest form of thinking is thinking without hypotheses. This "certain knowledge" only comes when the mind is calm. During sleep, for example, answers to particular questions can rise to the surface of our consciousness.

LINE OF THE HEAD AND LINE OF THE HEART CROSS EACH OTHER

Here, the line of the Head (see the illustration) runs upwards towards Mercury, indicating an extreme narrowing of consciousness. Emotional and intellectual powers cross each other and thinking then takes place at the expense of feeling. People with such crossing lines desire to achieve results in life (the influence of Mercury) by means of their intellectual powers. As just stated, these results are achieved at the expense of feeling. These people often go about their business in a cold, unfeeling manner.

LINES OF THE HEAD, HEART, AND LIFE ARISE AT THE SAME HEIGHT AND RUN TOGETHER FOR A SHORT DISTANCE

The energies are now joined together (see the illustration), creating such a tension that violent outbursts can easily occur. In the past (in a previous life) all these energies were drawn together and, at that moment, these people experienced thinking, feeling, and the resulting physical reaction all at the same time; these people are still locked in that situation.

LINE OF THE HEAD FORKS AT THE END

A fork at the end of a line shows that there is more than one way of applying the energy from that line. The positive aspect of this is that we can choose between two possibilities. The negative aspect, however, is that often we do not know which way to choose.

The fork at the end of the Head line (see the illustration) indicates a choice between two forms of thinking: analytic or creative. People with this line then usually either choose one or the other, or first use one form and then the other. The best option, of course, is some kind of synthesis. The two powers are then in harmony with each other.

AN ISLAND IN THE LINE OF THE HEAD

An island in a line tells us that the energies of that line were blocked for a certain period of time.

An island in the line of the Head (see the illustration) indicates that the person has experienced difficulties with intellectual functioning. But the line continues after the island, which shows that the problems have been overcome.

A BROKEN LINE OF THE HEAD

This indicates that the thought energy of these people has been undirected for a certain period of time. When the line begins again, they have found a direction of thought. Often such a line begins a little lower or a little higher than the original line (see the illustration). This points to the fact that their thinking has received a new impulse in order to continue on another level. During this period, these people can experience strong feelings of uncertainty.

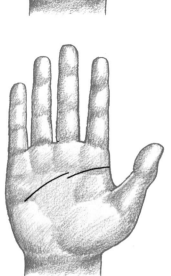

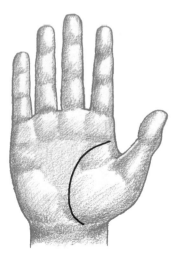

The Line of Life

Key words: physical power
life energy
life span

Indications for all those facets concerned with our life force can be found in this line (see the illustration). In the first place, we can read the state of our health from the line of Life as well as the degree of our stamina and physical strength. Interruptions in the stream of life—such as illnesses and unpleasant events—also leave their traces in this line.

This line also indicates our attitude to life—whether we face life in an enthusiastic, hesitant, depressive, or positive manner. In short, the line of Life is an indication of the path we tread through life. It shows with what energy and devotion we do it, and what aims we are striving for. In the *Hasta Samudrika Shastra,* the line of Life is called the line of *jeevan* (life force).

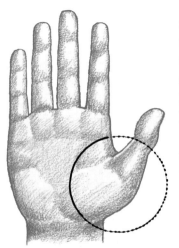

This life force can be compared to a circle (see the illustration). When we incarnate, the tap of life opens, so to speak, and the life force flows again. When we depart this earthly life, the tap is turned off. The dotted line that completes the circle indicates our existence in another dimension. If the tap is fully open, our energy flows in abundance. Sometimes, however, the flow slows to a trickle, and now and again, because of illness or some other event, it almost ceases.

NORMAL CIRCLE

This line of Life (see the illustration) forms an almost perfect circle without interruptions. This indicates a longing for a harmonious life.

People with such a line want to live pleasurably, and they are often successful in this aim, because the Mount of Venus gives them the space to do so.

LINE OF LIFE HAS A FLAT CURVE

When this line has a flat curve, the Mount of Venus is constricted. Thus, people with such a line do not live so intensely, but more superficially.

They attempt to go through life without too much effort or trouble. And that is impossible, of course, because life is full of obstacles to be overcome.

These people often do not see that taking an interest in and participating in the cultural and other good aspects of this world can improve the quality of their life. They therefore have few interests. They give up far too easily and try to harvest the fruits of deeds that they have not actually fully accomplished. Neither do they enjoy life to the full, because the Mount of Venus is restricted by the narrow curve of the line of Life.

If the Line of Life begins rather flatly and then becomes wider, it indicates a positive development. These people have obviously realized in time that they must exert themselves more in order to improve the quality of their life.

LINE OF LIFE HAS A VERY WIDE CURVE

People with such a line of Life (see the illustration) generally want too much. They have a huge appetite for life and pleasure. It would be sensible for them to take things easier and to bring a little more balance into their life.

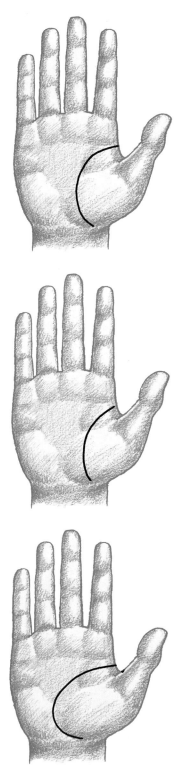

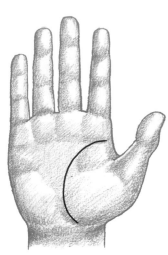

LINE OF LIFE ARISES BETWEEN MARS NEGATIVE AND THE MOUNT OF JUPITER

The ideal line of Life (see the illustration) arises between Mars negative and the Mount of Jupiter. Here, the energies of both mounts flow together in the line of Life. Mars negative, in particular, supplies physical energy to the line.

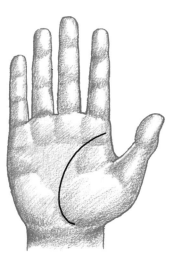

LINE OF LIFE ARISES IN JUPITER

People with this line of Life (see the illustration) are ambitious and their ambition is particularly directed to the physical aspects of life. They may want to become a major league baseball star, for example, and they set about achieving this goal in a most ambitious way. Despite this dynamic exertion, however, there is no harmony between their emotional and mental qualities. As a result, people with such a line quickly become unsettled if they do not achieve their goals.

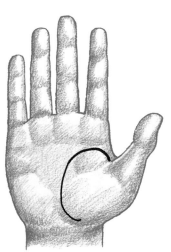

LINE OF LIFE ARISES IN MARS NEGATIVE

The life force and the attitude to life of people with such a line (see the illustration) are directed to earthly matters. They chiefly concern themselves with the physical aspects of life and, for example, happily perform physical labor.

LINE OF LIFE ENDS IN VENUS

If the line of Life ends in Venus (see the illustration), there is a harmonious life force. People with such a line are family-oriented, and when their family line is harmonious, they are very much home-lovers.

LINE OF LIFE ENDS BETWEEN VENUS AND LUNA

People with this line of Life (see the illustration) will make every effort to improve their karma. In other words, by means of their own exertions, they will strive to restructure the negative results of their past actions into positive results.

If, for example, we have idled our way through a number of lives, we must then work extremely hard for a few lives in order to restore a balance. People with such a line of Life are prepared to work hard and long in this life in order to achieve karmic balance.

If these people have a short thumb, however, the intention to achieve balance is present, but they lack the motivation to implement it.

LINE OF LIFE ENDS DEEP IN LUNA

Such a line of Life (see the illustration) indicates that the life force is diversified. People with such a line are therefore restless and concern themselves with a variety of activities. They particularly seek adventure and sensation. But in this search, they do not come in contact with their "higher self." They charge about the world, obviously not yet realizing that the most important adventure is one's own inner growth and development.

This line also indicates a love of travelling. If such people also have a well-developed Luna and spatulate hands they may, for example, become explorers.

If this line ends less deeply in Luna, these qualities are weakened.

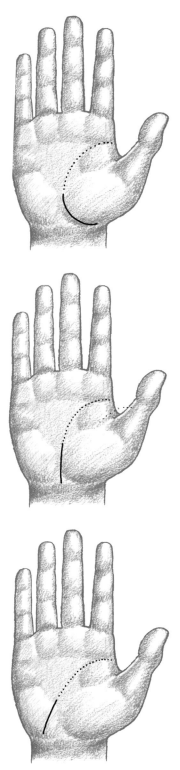

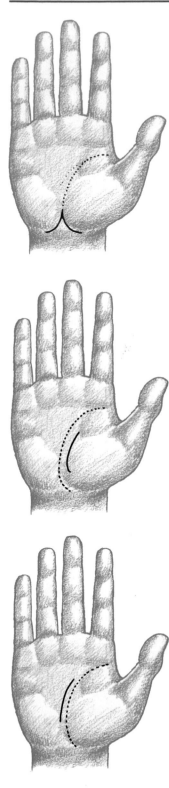

BRANCHING AT THE END OF THE LINE OF LIFE

These people want security and at the same time want to satisfy their longing for adventure. For example, they may emigrate to another country and immediately create a home with a nice garden.

It also frequently occurs that these people talk continually about emigration but never do anything concrete about it. They compensate for this by frequent travelling.

LINE OF MARS RUNS INSIDE OR OUTSIDE LINE OF LIFE

If the line of Mars runs inside the line of Life (see the illustration), it indicates that the life force seeks support. In a woman, this often means that she wants a partner who can offer her daily support in her life. If this wish is not fulfilled, she will feel that something is missing in her life. In a man, however, the line of Mars running inside the line of Life suggests additional life force. In this respect, the woman is the "receptive pole" and the man the "dynamic pole."

If the line of Mars runs outside the line of Life (see the illustration), it is a line of reinforcement. This line is also known as the sister line of the line of Life. People with such an extra line are more dynamic than people without it. Usually they need this extra strength because there is something amiss with their line of Life. Their life force may be interrupted or irregular. Such people may overcome some crisis with the aid represented by this line.

SHORT LINE OF LIFE

A short line of Life (see the illustration on the opposite page) does not necessarily indicate a short life span. However, it could indicate that a little while before birth we suddenly lost interest in a new life. But as soon as we began to enjoy life and to make ourselves useful, we regained our interest in life. The line of Life can then begin to grow again.

It may also have occurred that before our incarnation we did not know to which end we should use our life force. In the course of our life, however, we discovered a purpose for our life force and developed a desire to live longer as well. The free will of human beings plays a very important role on the stage of life.

INTERRUPTED LINE OF LIFE

An interrupted line of Life (see the illustration) indicates that for a number of years these people did not know how they should use their life force. During this period, they were unable to see the aim of their life clearly. The search, however, is now over and they have learned to use their life force purposefully.

An interrupted line of Life can also indicate a past illness, during which the life force could not flow freely.

With a purposeful life and a healthy life-style, breaks in the future do not necessarily have to materialize.

INTERRUPTION INSIDE

This line (see the illustration) indicates that a change has taken place (or will take place) in one's life. This change was concerned with a reduced (and therefore negative) use of energy and the quality of life was diminished. The faculty of free will can, in this case, also influence events.

INTERRUPTION OUTSIDE

This line (see the illustration) also indicates a change, but here the energy was (or will be) used positively in order to live a fuller life.

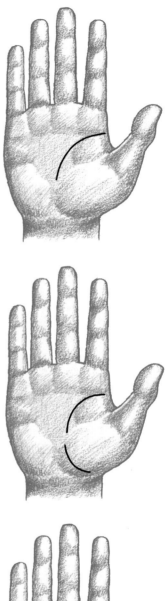

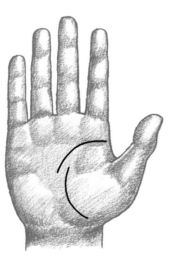

8·SECONDARY LINES

In contrast to the primary lines, which represent the unconscious mind, the secondary lines reflect the conscious mind. The secondary lines are linked with awareness of self and with free will. These lines are not etched so deeply because they lie close to our consciousness. Therefore, the secondary lines can change more easily than the primary lines, which have taken a long time to form. The deeper the secondary lines are etched in our hand, however, the stronger the inclination to follow a particular pattern of behavior.

Girdle of Venus

Key words: creativity of the spirit
energy source for emotional balance

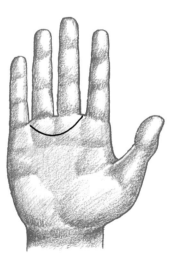

The Girdle of Venus (see the illustration) is an indication of the creativity of the spirit. In terms of relationships, people with a well-developed Girdle of Venus connect with others in a warm, meaningful, conscious, and ethical manner in order to achieve spiritual love.

In the *Hasta Samudrika Shastra,* the Girdle of Venus is known as *pranay,* which means "feeling of love." In evolutionary hand analysis, the Girdle of Venus is the line of the awakening soul. If we have a Girdle of Venus in our hand, our capacity for love has been purified and has attained a high level.

The intention in evolution is to achieve an increasingly higher and purer form of love. Pure love makes us spontaneous and from spontaneity arises creativity. Because we have a physical body, we are able to give this creativity form in the physical world.

People with a well-formed Girdle of Venus are therefore creative and have the capacity to express their creativity aesthetically and with refinement.

THE IDEAL GIRDLE OF VENUS

The ideal Girdle of Venus arises between Jupiter and Saturn and ends between Apollo and Mercury (see the illustration).

For the sake of clarity, let us now divide the hand into two "worlds": the "inner world" and the "outer world." Now let us imagine a line that divides these two worlds. The inner world is then represented by the thumb, Jupiter, and Saturn, and the outer world by Apollo and Mercury.

The ideal Girdle of Venus joins the qualities of the thumb (the "I"), Jupiter (ego), and Saturn (introversion) with the qualities of Mercury and Apollo (extroversion). One can say that the "inner" is carried to the "outer" by the Girdle of Venus.

GIRDLE OF VENUS WITH ENDS IN JUPITER AND MERCURY

People with such a Girdle of Venus (see middle illustration) have a tendency to manifest their creativity too much, without sufficiently going inside themselves to recharge their creative energy.

If the Girdle of Venus is in the correct position on one side of the hand yet runs too far to the outside of the other side (see bottom illustration), then these people think deeply and creatively, but they still express themselves too enthusiastically and in so doing arouse opposition.

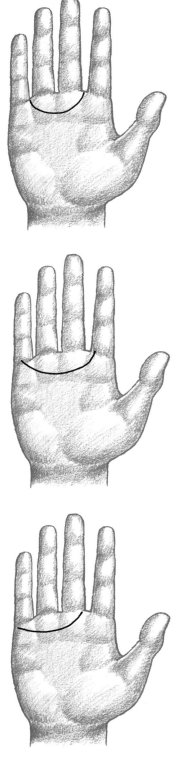

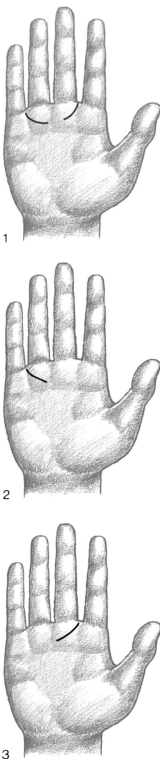

1

2

3

GROWING GIRDLE OF VENUS

A growing Girdle of Venus (see illustration 1) indicates a growing consciousness. In these people, the soul is trying to develop in order to express the higher values of life in a loving manner. As soon as this struggle has been won, the lines grow towards each other. The Girdle of Venus can also grow just on one side.

If the Girdle of Venus grows on the side of Mercury and Apollo (see illustration 2), it indicates that the person is developing from the "outside" to the "inside." Such people are favorably influenced by outside occurrences that bring their inner self to life. The layers concealing their being, as it were, are peeled away to reveal a pure inner core.

If the Girdle of Venus grows on the side of Saturn and Jupiter (see illustration 3), it indicates that the person is developing from the "inside" to the "outside." The growth of the soul occurs through the person's own impulses and not from influences from the outside.

NO GIRDLE OF VENUS

It can also occur, of course, that no Girdle of Venus is present, but this does not always mean that people without this line have not achieved a high level of evolution. A high level has often been reached and this can be seen in the rest of the hand. This high level, however, has not yet manifested in practice. One of the reasons we are on this earth is to learn to manifest the qualities of our soul.

GIRDLE OF VENUS TAKES OVER LINE OF THE HEART

A length of the line of the Heart is missing in people with such a Girdle of Venus (see the illustration on the opposite page). This indicates that in a previous life, they had probably lost heart as a result of a traumatic event, or that they have remained locked in a crisis situation. Because of this, the Heart line has disappeared.

The energy reflected in the Girdle of Venus is of a higher vibration than that reflected in the line of the Heart. Therefore, people with such a Girdle of Venus face life with a greater sensitivity as well as refinement.

People with such a line can function adequately although emotional tensions often create problems for them. This is because the Girdle of Venus is not intended to absorb emotional tensions.

Paradoxically, because they are so sensitive, such people sometimes appear insensitive and hard, since they tend to control their emotions with their intellect as a self-defense mechanism.

BROKEN GIRDLE OF VENUS

A broken Girdle of Venus (see the illustration) is a sign of growth. People with this broken line are trying to bring the different dimensions of their life into harmony with each other. They have attained a high level but have not yet been able to anchor themselves firmly at that level. The expression of altruistic love will assist them in this growth process.

ISLAND IN THE GIRDLE OF VENUS

An island in a line points to a block in the energy flow. An island in the Girdle of Venus (see the illustration) indicates that there is a disruption in the refinement of the creative expression of the soul.

THERE IS A GIRDLE OF VENUS IN THE LEFT HAND BUT NOT IN THE RIGHT HAND

This indicates that we have the opportunity to develop the qualities of the Girdle of Venus further in this life provided that we take the trouble to do so.

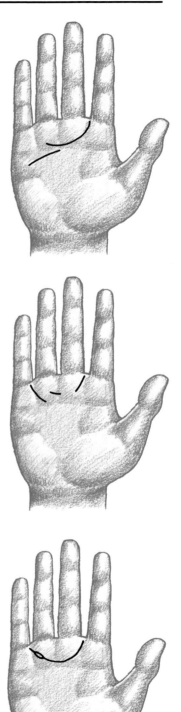

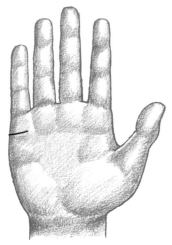

The Line(s) of Affection

Key words: love life
        romance

The line of Affection—sometimes referred to as the line of Relationship—is found under the little finger. This location is also connected with the heart meridian (a meridian is a subtle energy channel) and affection and marriage are, of course, affairs of the heart.

The line of Affection indicates that at a certain age there is a tendency to enter into a relationship. Lines of Affection do not always yield accurate information, however, because we have the free will to make our own decisions. If, for example, a hand contains three lines of Affection, it does not necessarily indicate that that person will enter into three steady relationships or marriages during his or her lifetime. The inclination can be seen in the hand, but that person may, for various reasons, remain with one partner. Because of this, lines of Affection must be considered in relation to other lines in the hand.

The higher intention of a relationship is for both partners to learn to unite the inner woman (anima) and the inner man (animus) within themselves. A partner is often a reflection of our own inner man or woman. Therefore, a relationship is actually a process of two people growing both together and individually.

I hesitated before deciding to include an explanation of the line(s) of Affection because an inexpert application of such information could cause a great deal of damage. I thus ask you to practise care and common sense in the study of this line.

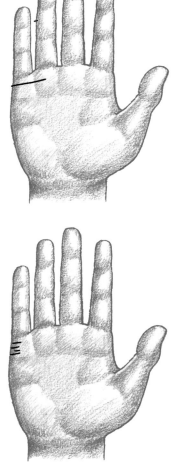

DEEPLY ETCHED LINE OF AFFECTION

Such a line indicates a deep relationship.

THIN LINE OF AFFECTION

The relationship of people with a thin line of Affection are not so deep and intense. This may occur in people whose parents decided on their marriage partner.

LONG LINE OF AFFECTION

People with a long line of Affection have the potential to enter into a long-term relationship.

When the line of Affection runs to a position under Apollo (see the top illustration), the relationship takes on the vibrations of the heart, so to speak. There is a tremendous unity between the partners and such a relationship can be extremely happy.

These people have been together for many lives: a karmic and truly blessed union.

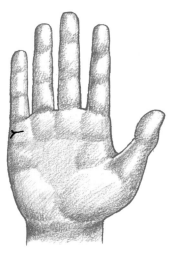

MANY THIN LINES

People with such lines of Affection (see the illustration) have a strong desire for a satisfactory relationship but try to satisfy that desire by taking several partners.

If several thin lines and a thick line can be seen, it shows that that person probably has a steady relationship but does not place a high premium on marital fidelity.

A FORK WHERE THE LINE ARISES

This line (see the illustration) indicates that a relationship has begun for the wrong reasons.

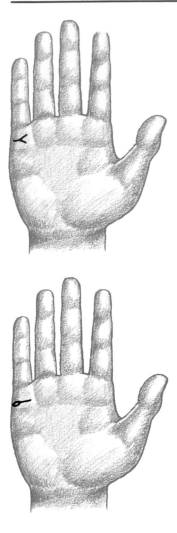

For example, one partner may have met the other when that partner had just come out of a relationship and wanted to marry again out of loneliness. This, naturally, is not a good basis for a relationship. Or, the partners may have fundamentally different outlooks on life.

People with this line need to be aware of their own and their partner's motives, and should examine their choices carefully.

A FORK WHERE THE LINE ENDS

People with a fork at the end of the line of Affection (see the illustration) often live with a partner who has distinctly different opinions.

AN ISLAND WHERE THE LINE ARISES

An island where the line arises (see the illustration) indicates that there is a possibility that a relationship may fail, despite there being a great attraction between the partners.

Nonetheless, if the line is deep enough, the relationship can still be successful.

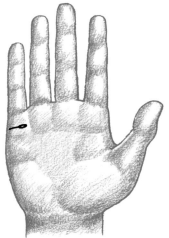

AN ISLAND WHERE THE LINE ENDS

An island where the line ends (see the illustration) indicates that the relationship has ended or will end in the future. The ending of the relationship usually involves disputes and arguments.

AN ISLAND IN THE MIDDLE OF THE LINE

An island in the middle of the line of Affection (see the illustration) indicates a period of disruption in the relationship. This crisis has been overcome, however, and with fresh heart both partners have entered a new phase of the relationship.

THE LINE CURVES UPWARDS

Such a line (see the illustration) suggests a longing for freedom within a relationship. This longing is not neurotic, however. The line of Affection curves upwards and reaches for the cosmos. These people seek spiritual freedom and in their relationship this longing is reflected in freedom from attachment. They understand that partners do not always have to be physically together in order to have a strong, spiritual bond. These people often do not see the necessity of marriage.

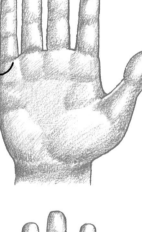

LINE OF AFFECTION RUNS DIAGONALLY DOWNWARDS

The restrictions imposed by a relationship weigh heavily on people with such a line (see the illustration). For this reason, they do not have a carefree, joyful marriage or relationship, but rather experience it as a heavy burden.

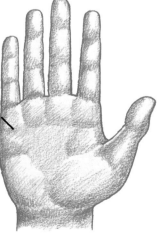

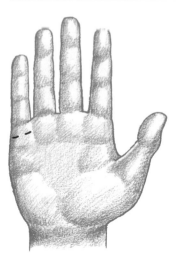

A BROKEN LINE OF AFFECTION

A broken line connotes a temporary break in a relationship, but with a chance that the partners will get together again (see the illustration).

LINE OF AFFECTION ENDS IN A PERPENDICULAR LINE

Such a line (see the illustration) indicates that the relationship is finished and that the partners can no longer be reconciled.

VERTICAL LINES THROUGH THE LINE OF AFFECTION

People with lines such as these (see the illustration) have a tendency to argue continually. They are still together with their partner but frequently cause disputes. These disputes are usually major because each partner adheres to different fundamental points of view.

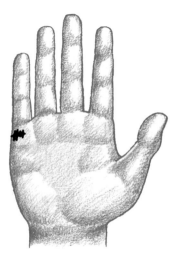

THIN LINE OF AFFECTION NEXT TO A THICK LINE

In addition to their primary relationship, these people have another, very intimate relationship, which can be spiritual or physical in nature.

It can also occur that people with such lines only yearn for such an intimate relationship (see the illustration).

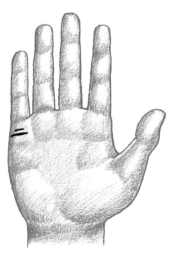

LINES OF AFFECTION ARE FOUND IN THE SAME PLACE IN BOTH HANDS

If the line of Affection in the left hand is short and that in the right hand is long (see the illustration), it indicates that the person is determined, through tenacity and perseverance, to overcome the difficulties in a relationship.

The short line of Affection in the left hand signifies that these people (in a former life) have not worked hard enough on a relationship. Now (in this life) the line of Affection in the right hand is longer, which means that they have learned not to give up so quickly, and this enables them to enter into a longer term relationship.

If the line of Affection in the left hand is long and that in the right hand short, it means that these people have been together in former lives but have not concluded their relationship. They must now accomplish that last phase.

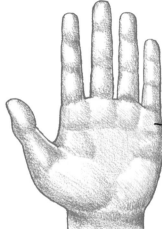
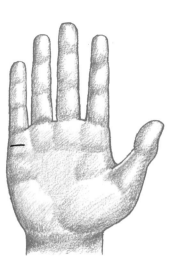

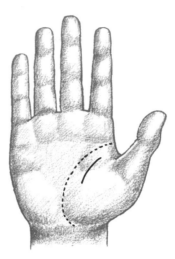

Line of Mars

Key words: physical strength
life energy
support from others

The line of Mars originates in Mars negative (see the illustration), the mount that (as already discussed) represents our life force and physical powers. This line runs inside the Life line and supports it.

In women, this support generally takes the form of a relationship. A partner—or perhaps a father or a friend—helps them along the path of life.

In men, the line of Mars usually signifies a strengthening of the life force. Mars negative provides additional energy so that they can travel along the path of life with extra vitality. As discussed earlier, in this respect women are more dependent than men and are able to attract supporting power. In general, men are more decisive and dynamic and therefore have less need of this support.

If, however, the anima (the inner feminine powers) are well developed in a man, the line of Mars has the same function as it has in a woman. The man then also seeks the support of others. The reverse is also true. If a woman has a strongly developed animus (the inner masculine powers), she has less need of support.

We use the term "feminine hand" when the hand has a conic or psychic shape and the Mount of Luna and the Mount of Venus are well developed. The following explanations for the different lines of Mars are valid only for the feminine-hand form.

In reading the line of Mars, it is also important to look at the line of Affection. Diagnostic hand analysis is a science that provides the most accurate explanation possible by combining indications from various features of the hand.

LINE OF MARS RUNS INWARD (FEMININE HAND)

People whose line of Mars runs inward (see the illustration) experienced support at the beginning of their life. This is indicated by the line of Mars running close to the line of Life. This support disappeared at a later stage in their life, however, which is indicated by the line of Mars running at an increasing distance from the line of Life. This can occur when the supporting partner slowly grows away from them or when they themselves have less and less need of support in their everyday life.

LINE OF MARS ARISES AT THE SIDE OF THE HAND AND THEN ENDS (FEMININE HAND)

People with such a line of Mars had a great deal of support at the beginning of their life. Their parents, for example, might have given them an excellent start in life. However, this support is known to fade at a later stage.

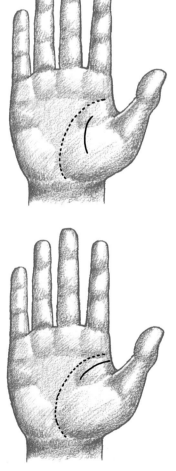

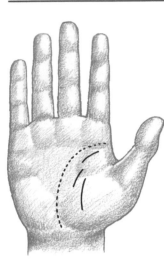

A FEW LINES OF MARS (FEMININE HAND)

These people experience a lot of support. When one means of support disappears, another takes its place.

If these lines are situated at a distance from the Life line (see the illustration), the support is not experienced in a very physical manner. Such people might, for example, receive letters from another country—from someone who is supporting them from a distance.

LINE OF MARS INTERSECTS LINE OF LIFE (FEMININE HAND)

The line of Mars intersecting the line of Life (see the illustration) is not a favorable sign. This is because it indicates that the energy flow of one partner is disrupting the life force of the other, and this indicates conflict and domination.

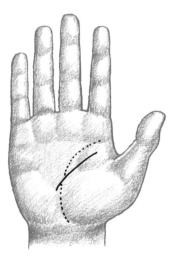

People with such a line must take great care in choosing a life partner. The formation of these lines points to a disharmonious relationship.

LINE OF MARS WITH AN ISLAND (FEMININE HAND)

When there is an island in the line of Mars (see the illustration), it indicates that the person's partner is going through a wretched period. He or she is experiencing a crisis (a block) and this influences the relationship. Such an island can appear over a period of just a few months. However, as soon as the crisis is over, this sign also disappears from the hand of the partner.

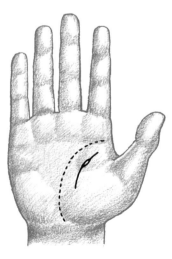

If the island is positioned at the beginning of the line of Mars, it indicates that initially the support of the partner was not offered for reasons of disinterest. People with such an island should therefore take into account that certain difficulties may arise at the beginning of a relationship. The island forms before these difficulties actually manifest because they are anticipated by the superconsciousness.

LINE OF MARS ARISES IN A FORK (FEMININE HAND)

This line indicates that at the beginning of the relationship, both partners are not "pulling together." In other words, they are a long way from reaching unanimity. Nonetheless, after the squabbling is resolved, they will be able to make a success of their relationship (see the illustration).

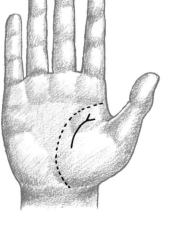

TRIANGLE IN THE LINE OF MARS (FEMININE HAND)

In people with a triangle in the line of Mars (see the illustration) the support of their partner is coupled with a good deal of wisdom.

CROSS IN THE LINE OF MARS (FEMININE HAND)

A cross (see the illustration) indicates that the relationship is going through a difficult period.

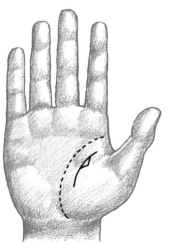

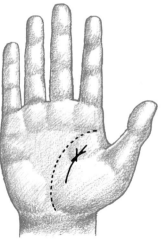

LINE OF MARS ARISES IN LINE OF LIFE (FEMININE HAND)

People whose line of Mars arises in their line of Life (see the illustration) generally feel closely linked to their partner. In such cases, we can speak of "two hearts beating as one."

   This line also often indicates that these people were together in previous lives. They are now together again, following the same current of life. Although recognition of their past lives together is not always present at the beginning of the relationship, these people nevertheless experience a deep feeling of oneness.

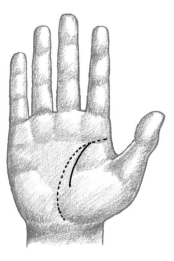

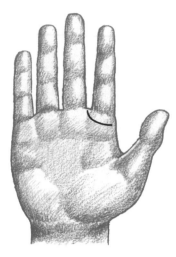

The Ring of Solomon

Key words: wisdom
altruistic love

Solomon was a wise king in biblical times; thus, this line (see the illustration) is a reflection of inner wisdom. It indicates an ability to reason at the highest level.

The idealism of Jupiter has ripened into love and wisdom and people with such a line have the capacity to put these qualities into practice. This line therefore reflects a higher form of love.

In the *Hasta Samudrika Shastra,* this line is known as *guru rekha.* The word *guru* means "he who dispels the darkness." People with such a line put themselves at the service of mankind and share cosmic universal love with others.

The Ring of Solomon is also a sign of advanced evolution.

THE RING OF SOLOMON RUNS ALONG THE UNDERSIDE OF THE MOUNT OF JUPITER

People with such a ring (see the illustration) have an altruistic type of love that is expresed in a physical manner. They may be very good at massage, for example.

If the line runs completely over the raised part of the mount, it indicates that these people have not completely freed themselves from feelings of lust. Although their consciousness has a higher aim, they still feel a desire for the pleasures of the flesh.

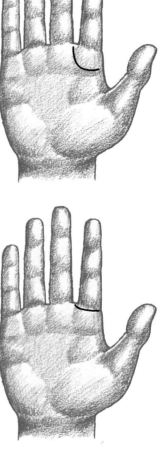

RING OF SOLOMON RUNS ALONG THE UPPER SIDE OF THE MOUNT OF JUPITER

When the ring runs along the upper side of the Mount of Jupiter (see the illustration), it indicates that these people have the capacity to express altruistic love in a mental way. They may be psychologists, for example.

RING OF SOLOMON RUNS ACROSS THE CENTER OF THE MOUNT OF JUPITER

In people with such a ring (see the illustration), both the intellectual and physical aspects of altruistic love are united. This means that they are often extremely good at social work. In its purest form, social work involves assisting and advising others without seeking any reward for one's own efforts. People who are involved with the problems of the Third World often have such a ring.

This ring is also known as the "ring of renunciation" because people with such a ring have the capacity to free themselves from attachment to "worldly pleasures."

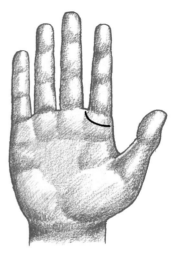

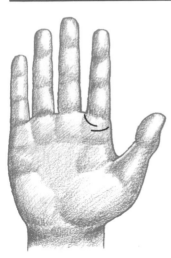

BROKEN RING OF SOLOMON

In people with such a broken ring (see the illustration), the energy needed to disseminate altruistic love is fragmented. The Ring of Solomon is a reflection of the harmony within ourselves, and if we do not possess this harmony, we are unable to pass it on to others. People with such a line attempt, as it were, to acquire this harmony from various perspectives, but they have not yet been successful in welding these powers into a unified force.

THIN RING OF SOLOMON

A thin line (see the illustration) indicates that one's level of altruisitc love has been reached only tentatively. The powers have not yet had the chance to develop fully.

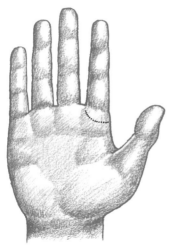

AN ISLAND IN THE RING OF SOLOMON

An island in the Ring of Solomon (see the illustration) indicates that there is a disruption (block) in the expression of the desire to assist others. These people feel the desire to express their love, but they are unable to do so. In many cases, such an island indicates frustrations in attempts to serve others.

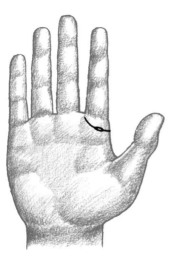

A THIN RING OF SOLOMON AND A HIGH MOUNT OF JUPITER

Among other things, Jupiter represents pride, and pride is the opposite of altruistic love. In people with an over-developed finger of Jupiter, the Ring of Solomon cannot develop further.

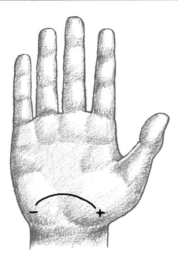

Via Lascivia

Key words: sexual disposition
              capacity to liberate oneself from sexual
              obsession

This line (see the illustration) can run from the positive pole of Venus to the negative pole of Luna. From Venus the line first runs upwards and then loops downwards to Luna. This is the area of the reptilian brain, where our instincts dominate and our sexual drive is situated.

People with such a line therefore tend to be interested in the sexual aspects of life. Their sexual pleasure, however, is often linked with financial profit. Prostitutes of both sexes sometimes possess such a line.

VIA LASCIVIA DOES NOT COMPLETELY CURVE DOWN INTO LUNA

People with such a line do not know exactly how they should behave sexually. They are still trying to liberate themselves, which is indicated by the line not fully curving down into Luna. They have not yet been able to free themselves completely from their compulsive sexual desires.

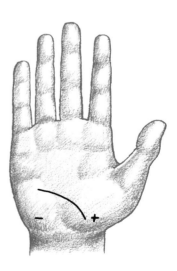

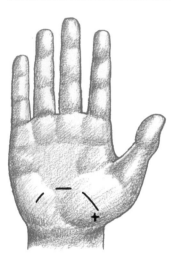

BROKEN VIA LASCIVIA

People with this broken line (see the illustration) indulge their sexual impulses on one occasion, but not on the next. They are uncertain about this aspect of their life.

VIA LASCIVIA AND GIRDLE OF VENUS IN ONE HAND

Here, the Via Lascivia cancels out the purity of the Girdle of Venus, since negative elements usually dominate the positive. These people almost always experience problems in their relationships. They are used by others and, at the same time, use others. This goes against their inner refinement (Venus), arousing feelings of unrest.

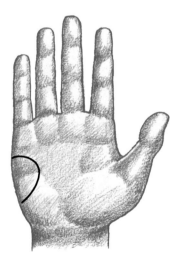

Line of Intuition

Key words: receptivity
               psychic capacities

This line (see the illustration) runs from Luna to Mars positive or Mercury. Luna represents the physical and the reception of impulses from the outside world. Mars positive and Mercury both represent intellectual and spiritual qualities. The line of Intuition therefore links the body with the spirit.

This line reflects an extroverted type of intuition. People who have it are able to penetrate the energy field of other people and in so doing sense what is going on inside them. This line, however, does not reflect any intuition we may have about ourselves.

How this extroverted intuitive capacity is handled (in a positive or a negative manner) can be seen from other signs in the hand.

INTERRUPTED LINE OF INTUITION

People with such a line (see the illustration) cannot yet take these capacities completely for granted. Sometimes they receive the right impressions and sometimes not. An interrupted line of Intuition indicates growth and a conscious attempt to develop in this area.

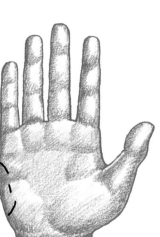

LINE OF INTUITION IS FLAT AND RUNS ALONG THE SIDE OF THE HAND

In people with such a line (see the illustration) the capacity for intuitive receptivity is still superficial. They must attempt to penetrate more deeply into the energy fields of other people.

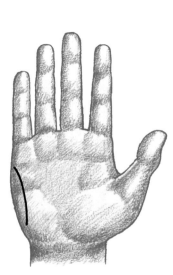

The Line of Karma, or of Destiny or Saturn

Key words: destiny in life
opposition on the path of life

The word "karma" has Sanskrit origins, and has as its root the word "kri," which means "action." The actions we took in previous lives had certain consequences, on which basis we now go forward. Karma is therefore concerned with the law of cause and effect. Now, in this life, we are encountering the effects of our creditable or discreditable actions with respect to our fellow men during previous lives. The law of karma, in its true sense, is the greatest dynamic power in Indian philosophy. Karma is also regarded as the creative force in Tibetan Buddhism.

Karma is the force that makes our life meaningful and that puts the responsibility for our life into our own hands. The effects of our deeds always have consequences in the future.

Vasanas (an Eastern concept) are left-over, unconscious influences from previous lives and the driving force of our creative potential. *Vasanas* can be growth-promoting or growth-limiting. For example, growth-promoting *vasanas* could be the positive effects of acts of courage or a spirit of enterprise in the past, and growth-limiting *vasanas* might be feelings of fear or anger retained from past experiences.

Diagnostic hand analysis, based on the *Hasta Samudrika Shastra,* gives us insight into the *vasanas* and indicates how we can free ourselves from those that are destructive by putting more energy behind those that promote growth.

People have free will, however limited that might be. The following analogy makes this clear: A cow is tied to a rope in the middle of a meadow. She does not have the freedom to graze the whole meadow, but she is free to move within the circle determined by the length of the rope. In other words, people have sufficient "space" to take their destiny—to a great extent—into their own hands. Therefore, the "line of Fate," which is sometimes used to describe this line, is an inaccurate term.

The French philosopher and writer Jean-Paul Sartre didn't believe in fatalism either and he expressed this succinctly when he said that "the opposite of free will is not determinism but fatalism."

The line of Karma, also called the line of Destiny or the line of Saturn, shows our destiny and the opposition we may meet on our path through life. Without opposition and exertion, there is no progress. It is only the resistance of the air that allows a bird to fly.

Saturn destroys our old habits by creating opposition in that we are compelled to learn new habits by overcoming difficulties. In Greek mythology, Saturn (Chronos) swallowed his children and he still does that with us mortals.

Fortunately, however, if, after difficult times, Saturn "coughs up" his children, the line of the Sun is prepared to reward work well done and to deliver fresh energy.

Each line that runs in the area of Saturn and towards the direction of Saturn (see the illustration) is a line of Karma. Various lines of Karma can be seen in our hand, representing our destiny in different areas, such as marriage or work.

Saturn swallowing his children (Rubens).

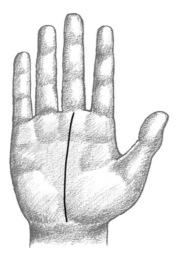

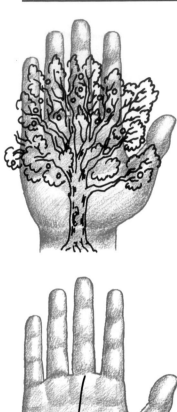

If we draw a tree in the hand (see the illustration), the forces from previous lives are on the side of the wrist. At the bottom of the hand are the roots of this life that are nourished by fertile or infertile soil. Energy flows from the roots to the branches by way of the trunk. It is here that the fruits of our actions grow. The fingers (as already stated) represent our conscious energy, which is unconsciously available in the palm. The line of Karma, or the line of Destiny, is therefore a continuing line from the past to the present and the future.

NO LINE OF KARMA

People without a line of Karma have no deeply felt conviction to follow particular directions in life. Often they do not see the deeper meaning in life. We can help these people by showing them the value of concentrated effort on the evolutionary path and by creating a destiny together with them.

Eventually, however, they must learn for themselves how to give substance to their life.

LINE OF KARMA RUNS THROUGH THE ENTIRE PALM FROM TOP TO BOTTOM

People with such a line of Karma (see the illustration) have a great need of security. They have a great desire for a well-ordered life and are therefore afraid of taking risks. They tend to hold on to certainties in this transitory life. The result of this, however, is that they have no certainty. If we are too eager to possess something, we do not obtain it. Life in its wisdom sometimes withholds certainty from us in order to teach us that absolute certainty can never actually be reached. The only certainty is that nothing is certain and that everything is subject to change.

LINE OF KARMA RUNS TOGETHER WITH LINE OF LIFE FOR A SHORT DISTANCE

Here, the powers of the line of Karma and the line of Life merge (see the illustration) and that creates a "short circuit." This short circuit is severe because the downward-flowing energy of the line of Life clashes with the upward-flowing energy of the line of Karma. Such a line, therefore, always points to difficult times and signifies a great deal of life energy being used in following one's destiny.

This collision of energy is coupled with emotional tension. The line of Karma is pulled towards the line of Life, and therefore towards Venus, which represents the way in which we deal with our emotions.

The challenge facing people with such a line of Karma is to overcome their emotional tensions.

LINE OF KARMA RUNS THROUGH LINE OF LIFE

This indicates that the energy of the line of Karma is overshadowed by intense efforts to handle emotions. Life, as it were, is pulled towards the limbic emotional part of the brain. This means that there is an almost unbearable tension in people who have such a line of Karma.

Once the line of Karma is released from the line of Life, these people are freed from their tension.

MORE THAN ONE LINE OF KARMA

People with lines like this (see the illustration) have different interests and different destinies on their path through life. The different lines of Karma, each in its turn, refer to various destinies. For example, one may have to do with marriage and another with work. The lines indicate the different paths these people can take.

A negative effect of several lines of Karma can be that one's energy is fragmented. The positive effect can be that one absorbs experiences from various areas of life.

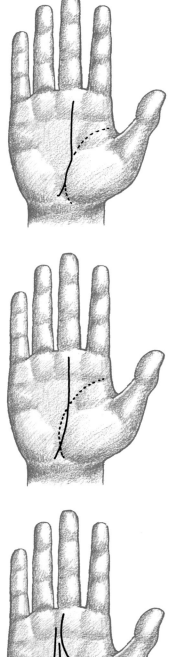

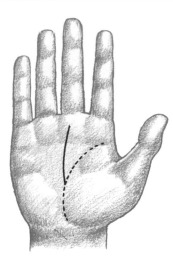

LINE OF KARMA ARISES IN LINE OF LIFE

At a particular point in their life, people with such a line (see the illustration) take their destiny into their own hands. The life current energizes their own initiative, giving them the power to choose and fulfill their own destiny.

LINE OF KARMA RUNS FROM LUNA

People whose line of Karma arises very deep in Luna (see the illustration) know that their destiny is to help others. This area, linked to the reptilian brain, gives them an instinctive urge to make themselves useful to other people.

If the line arises in the center of Luna (see the illustration), this feeling is emotionally charged, because this location is also connected to the limbic brain. People with such a line feel that they must be of service to others.

The stimuli from the senses enter through Luna; therefore, people with such a line of Karma are oriented towards others.

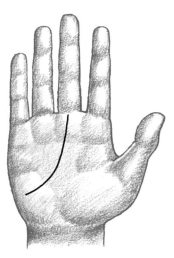

LINE OF KARMA STOPS AT LINE OF THE HEAD AND NO NEW LINES ARISE ABOVE IT

People with such a line (see illustration 1) had a goal and at a particular time fulfilled it.

It is also possible that they have broken off an activity through some injudicious action. Subsequently they found no further purpose and now wander aimlessly through life. These people must try to create a new purpose in their life.

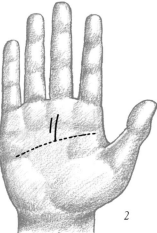

LINE OF KARMA ARISES IN LINE OF THE HEAD

This line (see illustration 2) indicates a change. New ideas originate from thought and these people will embark on new actions.

LINE OF KARMA STOPS AND AFTER A PERIOD GROWS IN A FINE FAN

People with such a line of Karma (see illustration 3) are subject to vacillation. They know that they must follow certain destinies but do not do so in practice.

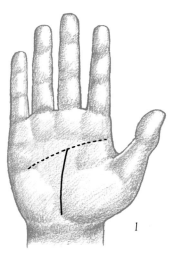

LINE OF KARMA STOPS AND THEN ARISES AGAIN A LITTLE HIGHER IN THE HAND

People with this line (see illustration 4) have lived for a period of time without a destiny. The potential to find a new destiny is present, however, as indicated by the line of Karma continuing higher in the hand.

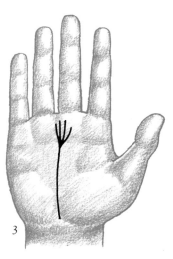

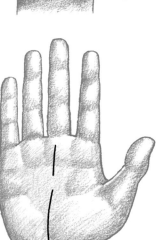

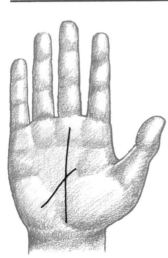

LINE OF KARMA IS CROSSED BY A LINE ARISING IN LUNA

When the line of Karma is crossed by a line arising in Luna (see the illustration), it indicates a disruption. Luna reflects romantic impulses (received through the senses). Therefore, this line shows that a romantic relationship can begin but eventually comes to nothing. Romanticism is, in essence, an illusion and this illusion is interrupted by the energy represented by the line of Karma.

In a feminine hand, these crossing lines often refer to a personal relationship, whereas in a masculine hand, they often refer to a business relationship.

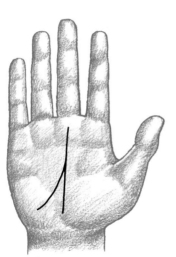

LINE OF KARMA MERGES WITH A LINE ARISING IN LUNA

Here, the two energies merge and flow onwards in a single line (see the illustration). Such a merging indicates that a personal or a business relationship will be very successful.

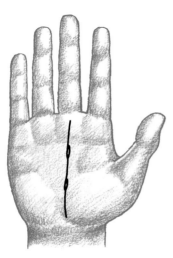

ISLANDS IN THE LINE OF KARMA

Islands indicate disruptions that must be handled. People with islands in the line of Karma (see the illustration) experience opposition from their immediate environment. The nature of these disruptions can be read from the mounts. As already stated, opposition gives us the opportunity to learn lessons in life.

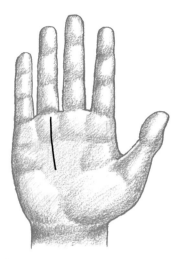

Line of the Sun, or of Apollo

Key words: prosperity
                popularity
                charm

As the line of Karma can be associated with exertion, the line of Apollo can be associated with relaxation. The line of Karma stands for the capital in the bank, as it were, and the line of Apollo the interest we obtain from it.

The line of Apollo represents the reward for all the positive efforts people have made in the past. In previous lives, they put their considerable qualities and talents towards the service of others, and now they can enjoy the finer side of life.

Therefore, this line represents various pleasurable facets, such as popularity, attractiveness, and charm. It also points to success and freedom from financial worries.

The line of Apollo is a vulnerable line that can easily be overshadowed by other—especially negative—forces in the hand. If people have the potential to receive rewards, for example, but the other forces in the hand work against that, they will not enjoy such rewards. They may have low self-esteem, reflected by an underdeveloped Mars negative, and feel that they are undeserving of rewards.

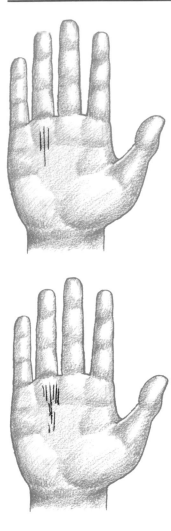

MORE THAN ONE LINE OF THE SUN

The line of the Sun runs in the area of the Mount of Apollo towards the finger of Apollo (see the illustration). People with more than one line have felt deeply the possibility of experiencing happiness in more than one area of life.

MANY LINES OF THE SUN

People with many lines of the Sun (see the illustration) have a great deal of sun energy. This means that they go about things in a very enthusiastic manner and want to handle many things at the same time.

Yet, because they have so many irons in the fire, their burden is too heavy and in the long run they actually achieve less. Their composure is disturbed because they are seeking fulfillment in too many areas and their energy is fragmented because they have too many interests.

These people must learn to crystallize their energy and follow only a few interests.

LINE OF THE SUN AND LINE OF KARMA ARISE AT APPROXIMATELY THE SAME HEIGHT

The line of the Sun and the line of Karma may arise at the same height. In this illustration, they arise in the line of the Head. It's likely that people with this combination will conceive an idea that will work out successfully. The line of the Sun indicates how people's undertakings satisfy them emotionally.

LINE OF THE SUN ARISES IN MARS POSITIVE

The mental exertions of people with such a line (see il-lustration 1) will be met with success. They must fight for their happiness and work very hard for it, however.

Mars positive attracts support from the outside; there-fore, these people are also offered help by others.

LINE OF THE SUN ARISES IN LINE OF THE HEART

Later in life these people have the potential to live in an emotionally harmonious manner (see illustration 2).

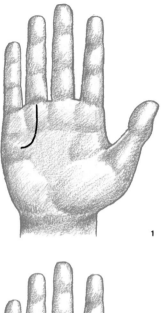

ISLAND IN THE LINE OF THE SUN

An island in the line of the Sun (see illustration 3) points to a deeply felt disappointment. The cause of this disap-pointment might be publicly known.

LINE OF THE SUN ARISES IN LINE OF KARMA

Such a line (see illustration 4) indicates that these people feel successful and satisfied in what they are doing. In professional terms, for example, this might indicate a promotion.

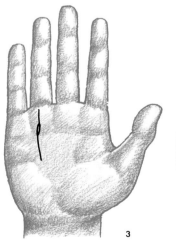

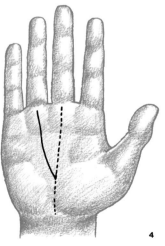

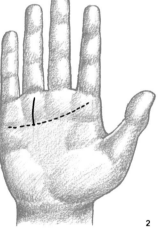

9·SIMPLE ANALYSIS

Here are simple analyses of three different right hands. (Keep in mind that the handprints are mirror images.)

MAN, 27 YEARS OLD

This is a square hand shape. The skin texture is rough and the lines are broad and shallow. The line of the Head is short. The line of the Heart arises between Jupiter and Saturn and runs in a shallow curve through the hand. There are double lines of Life, which are both connected

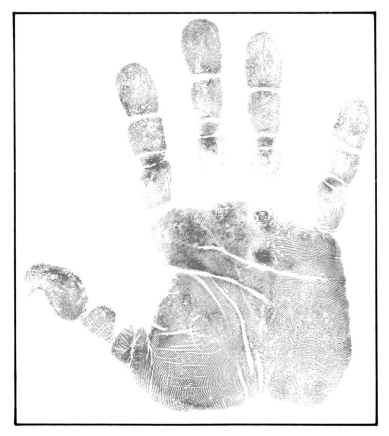

to the line of the Head. Almost no secondary lines can be seen in the hand. The thumb and the finger of Jupiter are short, whereas the finger of Apollo is long.

The square hand shape indicates an honest, practical, and trustworthy personality. The rough skin texture, as well as the broad, shallow lines, point to a physically oriented approach to life. The short line of the Head also signifies an interest in the material side of life. These indications, together with the lack of secondary lines, show that this man has little interest in the abstract or intellectual dimensions of life. The double line of Life allows much room for the Mount of Venus, which reflects his desire for a pleasurable life and physical pursuits.

The line of the Head merging with the two Life lines indicates that this man is timid and self-conscious. The short thumb and finger of Jupiter show that he has little motivation to make something of his life, which is also established by the short and vague line of Destiny. The line of the Heart, which begins between Jupiter and Saturn and curves only slightly, is indicative of his desire to enter into a serious relationship, in which sexual contact is important. The long finger of Apollo represents his good heart and his inner need to be of service to his fellow men. In essence, the whole hand gives an impression of a physical disposition without a great deal of motivation.

When this man came to me for a consultation, he was generally restless and unfocused. He said that he had a college education but did not know what he wanted to do with it. After reading this analysis, you can easily understand why this should be so.

In any case, I advised him to take up an occupation in which he could work physically in the outside world. He followed this advice and now works contentedly as a carpenter on construction sites. In the meantime, he has also married, and caring for his wife and children keeps him occupied. The influence of the long finger of Apollo is confirmed by the fact that since that first consultation, we have often discussed ways in which he can serve his colleagues.

WOMAN, 42 YEARS OLD

The hand is 80 percent square and 20 percent conic. The finger of Jupiter is overdeveloped. Mars negative is well-developed, as is the Mount of Luna. The line of the Heart begins high between Jupiter and Saturn and is beautifully curved.

The Girdle of Venus is beginning to form. The line of the Head has two branches. The upper branch runs towards Luna and the lower (broken) branch dips deep into Luna. The line of Life runs in a lovely curve to the center of the base of the hand. The line of Destiny ends at the line of the Head and a new line begins in this line. There are lines of Apollo in the hand, which become more pronounced after the line of the Heart.

The overdeveloped finger of Jupiter is the dominating force in this hand. It indicates that this woman is proud,

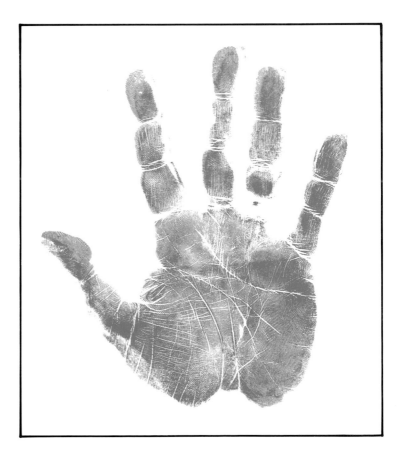

has a dogmatic attitude, and worries about the future. The line of the Heart connotes a soft, caring nature, and idealistic expectations regarding relationships. The upper branch of the line of the Head shows a receptive, creative way of thinking, and the lower branch a compulsive urge to maneuver herself into undesirable situations.

The line of Life indicates her desire to achieve continuous growth throughout her life. The well-developed Mount of Luna reflects her receptive nature and the well-developed Mars negative her positive self-esteem and healthy urge to manifest herself.

This woman entered a cloister, but the life of a nun did not agree with her. This can be read from the overdeveloped finger of Jupiter and the line of the Head that runs deep into Luna. An overdeveloped finger of Jupiter often indicates an attraction to organized religious services and this type of Head line frequently connotes people being brought into impossible situations.

This woman rebelled (as seen from the overdeveloped Jupiter), however, and left the cloister and married. All this is established by the line of Destiny that arises in the line of the Head. This line significes a new direction in life.

In the therapy I conducted with this woman, I helped her transform her excessive orientation to thinking (Jupiter) into a more balanced state between thinking and feeling.

I also helped her to transfer the energy from the lower branch of the line of the Head to the upper branch. This energy was shifted, as it were, from the reptilian brain to the limbic brain.

Now she is a good, motherly (Luna) therapist who has an instinctive feel (positive Luna, with the line of the Head running towards Luna) for people and is able to bring about healing. She has therefore been able to realize the potential reflected in the line of Apollo and has found satisfaction in her life.

MAN, 32 YEARS OLD

The most striking aspect of this hand is the Mount of Venus. This well-developed mount dominates the entire hand, thus indicating that this man is a true Venusian. The lines in the hand are deep and narrow. All the fingers and mounts are well-developed. Luna is rather short in relation to Venus, but this does not mean that it is underdeveloped. This characteristic reflects a more extroverted nature.

During our consultation, this man informed me that he had absolutely no problems. He was happily married and his political career was prospering. In short, he had achieved everything he had wanted to achieve, but he was very eager to know if I could give him any new insights. After a short examination of his hand, I concluded that his problem was the fact that he had no prob-

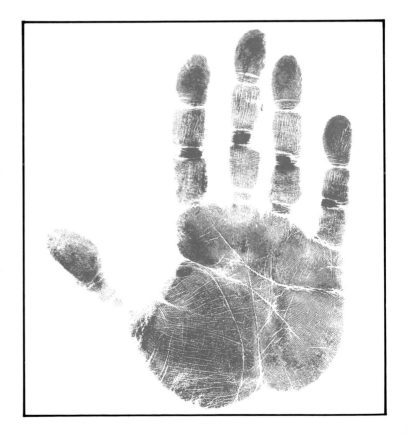

lems. He was "imprisoned" in his satisfaction. He possessed almost no neurotic properties of character that could spur him on to greater heights.

When people are so satisfied that it stagnates their spiritual growth, they often receive a shock in life that wakes them up. Such a shock could be read in this man's hand.

One of the indications was the island in the line of the Sun. Since this man was so pleasant—Venusians are always loving, friendly people—he didn't balk at my reading, even though I could see that my analysis had made little impression on him.

About a year later, his wife died under tragic circumstances. It was only after a considerable period of time and with great difficulty that he was able to see the lesson of life in this occurrence.

He is now completely involved in bringing groups of people together at an international level in order to create greater unity and fellowship. True Venusians like to see the whole world as one harmonious family.

10·MAKING HANDPRINTS

It is advisable to make two prints of both the left and right hands because a print may be indistinct or become lost. There are two methods of making handprints.

Method 1

MATERIALS

For the first method you need:

- a glass plate,
- fingerprint ink,
- a roller (such as a fairly hard paint roller or paperhanger's roller), and
- white paper.

TECHNIQUE

- Lay a sheet of white paper on a hard surface.
- Deposit a few drops of ink on the glass plate.
- Spread these drops smoothly over the plate with the roller.
- Pass the inked roller over the hand, ensuring that all the fingers and hollows are well-inked. To get the best results, use a light, evenly distributed layer of ink.
- Instruct the subject to place the hand on a sheet of white paper. This hand must be kept perfectly still, otherwise the print will be unclear.
- Press firmly down on the hand, without rolling, paying particular attention to the thumb, fingers, hollows, and palm.
- Hold the paper down; then ask the subject to remove the hand.

- Write on the paper the name and age of the subject and the date on which the print was made.

Method 2

MATERIALS

For method 2 you need:

- a special printing sheet (on which a thin layer of ink has been rolled),
- a roller (see method 1), and
- white paper.

TECHNIQUE

- Lay the special printing sheet on the hand.
- Roll out so that the ink is transferred to the hand.
- Continue as explained for Method 1.

*   *   *

The second method generally yields better results with less mess.

The ink can be removed with agents such as those mechanics use to clean their hands.

The purpose of making these prints is twofold. We can carefully study the details of the hand at leisure and we can compare the prints with prints made at a later date. When people change, the details in the hand also change.

"In Your Own Hand" Study Sheet

This is intended as a reference sheet, where you can enter all the hand analysis details of those whose hands you've read.

Indicate your observations with respect to color, temperature, skin, fingers and flexibility by making a cross in the appropriate squares. An exceptional nail shape can be drawn in the blank finger. The mounts and fingers can be indicated with plus or minus signs; the symbols have the following meanings:

w   = well-developed
−   = underdeveloped
− −   = very underdeveloped
+   = overdeveloped
+ +   = very overdeveloped

The under- or overdeveloped fingers can be drawn directly in the hand. The lines and characteristics can be drawn in both the blank hands.

Study Sheet

Name: . . . . | Man ☐ Woman ☐   Back

Address: . . . . | Date of Birth: . . . .

City, State, Zip Code: . . . . | Age: . . . .

Telephone: . . . . | left-handed ☐ right-handed ☐

<u>Color:</u>

Pink   ☐   . Mounts and

White   ☐   . Fingers

Yellow   ☐   . (++/+/w-/--)

Blue   ☐

Red   ☐

<u>Temperature:</u>

Cold   ☐

Normal   ☐

Warm   ☐

Hot   ☐

(links)

(Left)

<u>Skin:</u>

Rough   ☐

Average   ☐   Lines and

Fine   ☐   Characteristics

Very Fine ☐

<u>Fingers:</u>

Smooth   ☐

Average   ☐

Knotty   ☐

<u>Flexibility:</u>

Supple   ☐

Average   ☐

Stiff   ☐

Veins: . . . .   Other Characteristics: . . . .

Hand Shape: . . . . . .

INDEX